MARTHA STEWART'S
CRAFTS
FOR
KIDS

MARTHA STEWART'S
CRAFTS FOR KIDS

175 kids craft projects for weekends, rainy days and parties

photographs by Annie Schlechter and others

by the editors of Martha Stewart Living

D&C
David and Charles
www.stitchcraftcreate.co.uk

A DAVID & CHARLES BOOK

Copyright © Martha Stewart Living Omnimedia, Inc. 2013

Originally published in the United States by Potter Craft, an imprint of the Crown Publishing Group, a division of Random House, Inc., New York.
www.crownpublishing.com
www.pottercraft.com

First published in the UK in 2013 by David & Charles
David & Charles is an imprint of F&W Media International, Ltd
Brunel House, Forde Close, Newton Abbot, TQ12 4PU, UK
F&W Media International, Ltd is a subsidiary of F+W Media, Inc
10151 Carver Road, Suite #200, Blue Ash, OH 45242, USA

A catalogue record for this book is available from the British Library.

Potter Craft and colophon are registered trademarks of Random House, Inc.

Book and cover design by Gillian MacLeod
Cover photographs by Annie Schlechter

A list of photography credits appears on page 342

F+W Media publishes high quality books on a wide range of subjects. For more great book ideas visit: www.stitchcraftcreate.co.uk

ISBN-13: 978-1-4463-0374-0 PB
ISBN-10: 1-4463-0374-8 PB

Printed in United States of America by RR Donnelley for:
F&W Media International, Ltd
Brunel House, Forde Close, Newton Abbot, TQ12 4PU, UK

10 9 8 7 6 5 4 3 2 1

This book is dedicated to all the children of *Martha Stewart Living* employees. We hope that each and every child grows up crafting and creating, and we hope this book becomes a favorite guide.

CONTENTS

INTRODUCTION

This book could not come at a better time. My first grandchild, Jude Stewart, age two, sits down every day, several times a day, at a crafts table in her apartment, earnestly busying herself with numerous crafts projects appropriate for her age. She, like most children, is curious, active, interested, and unafraid of self-expression in almost any medium. She colors, finger-paints, pastes stickers everywhere, glues beans on paper, punches out interesting shapes like bunnies and flowers from colorful papers, and is just learning how to wield a paintbrush and color inside the lines. Much of what she will need for years to come, and what her mother will need to guide her, can be found right here in the pages of this book—including dozens of charming and easy projects, with step-by-step, clear how-to instructions. This book is, indeed, a treasure trove for children and their "teachers." The many various projects included were all designed with simplicity in mind, making good use of common materials, and encouraging colorful, happy, uncomplicated results. Nothing is so difficult that an attention span will wane, and nothing requires supplies that are difficult to find.

I was a crafter and artist as a child, always looking for a project that would result in something special to give to Mom, take to school, or display in our home. I painted, did lots of ceramics and pottery, and sewed, knitted, and embroidered. My list for Santa included art supplies, crafting tools, and papers and glues. My daughter, Alexis, was always busy—a diligent student, she also crafted constantly. She worked with clay, and she became an excellent weaver and potter. My many nieces and nephews were likewise occupied with crafts—many of which were inspired by teachers and homework assignments, but many originated at home, using supplies found in pantries and basement workshops. I was continually amazed at how prolific, how original, and how beautiful so many of their crafts were.

I have saved many one-of-a-kind objects given to me by young crafters—the painted and glazed clay bowls, the woven place mats and table runners, the paintings, the cards, the scarves, and the pot holders and the stuffed animals and necklaces and bracelets. I expect to be the recipient of many more such treasures as the result of this book, things that children of all ages will enjoy making after school, on weekends, and during holidays. I believe, as so many of us "doers" believe, that children need constant stimulation, continuous inspiration, and clear guidelines. They need projects for their hands as well as for their minds. Here are 175 excellent "recipes" to help them thrive.

Martha Stewart

P.S. To make a cross-stitch portrait like mine (opposite), see page 268.

ACKNOWLEDGMENTS

This fun-filled book is the brainchild of many talented people, all of whom share a common goal: to provide crafts ideas and inspiration for kids of all ages—and their grown-ups. Our team put this book together so that readers could spend quality time making, doing, and exploring together. Our crafts editors contributed brilliant ideas and boundless energy to the pages within, particularly Silke Stoddard, who always manages to surprise and delight us with her creativity. Thanks as well to all the many crafts editors of Martha Stewart Living Omnimedia, past and present, whose contributions made it into these pages, particularly Marcie McGoldrick, Jodi Levine, and Hannah Milman.

The Special Projects Group at Martha Stewart Living Omnimedia, led by Ellen Morrissey, collaborated with our resident crafts experts to compile the content on these pages. The top-notch team of editors—including Evelyn Battaglia, Amy Conway, and Susanne Ruppert—ensured that the step-by-step instructions for each project were accurate and easy to follow. Art and design directors Jennifer Wagner and Gillian MacLeod (whose lovely hand-drawn type adorns the cover and the chapter openers) created the book's winning design. As always, Editorial and Brand Director Eric A. Pike provided invaluable guidance every step of the way. Laura Wallis and Amber Mauriello lent their writing and editing skills. Jessi Blackham and Alexi Bullock assisted with art direction and design.

A million thanks to photographer Annie Schlecter, always a pleasure to work with, and to the other skilled photographers whose work graces these pages (a complete list of contributors appears on page 342). Thanks also to Anna Ross, Alison Vanek Devine, and John Myers for managing the voluminous imagery throughout the book, and to Denise Clappi and her team of imaging specialists, especially Kiyomi Marsh, for ensuring the quality of each one.

We are also grateful to a host of others who lent their time and talents, including Elizabeth Adler, Stephanie Fletcher, Davida Hogan, Laura Kaesshaefer, Kelsey Mirando, Benjamin Reynaert, and Deb Wood.

And a heartfelt thanks to all the adorable kids who eagerly contributed to the making of this book, among them: Renzo Battaglia, Hugo Kohnhorst, Nora Kohnhorst, Lucy Maguire, Henry Mitchell, Ella Schweizer, Emil Schweizer, and Lucas Stettner.

Finally, our deepest appreciation goes to our long-standing partners at Crown Publishers and Potter Craft—Victoria Craven, Alyn Evans, Derek Gullino, Pam Krauss, Maya Mavjee, Jess Morphew, Marysarah Quinn, Patricia Shaw, Eric Shorey, and Jane Treuhaft—for their support of and enthusiasm for this and all of our book publishing projects.

CHAPTER 1

CREATE a FEW CHARACTERS

Craft a bunch of playful pals with nothing more than some basic supplies and your imagination. These ideas give new meaning to the term "pet project."

ORIGAMI FINGER PUPPETS

Finger puppets are a snap to create with squares of paper and a set of markers. Make a few folds, and watch as the characters' personalities start to emerge; finish by drawing facial details. If you start with origami paper, which comes in convenient squares, you don't even have to do any cutting.

HOW-TO

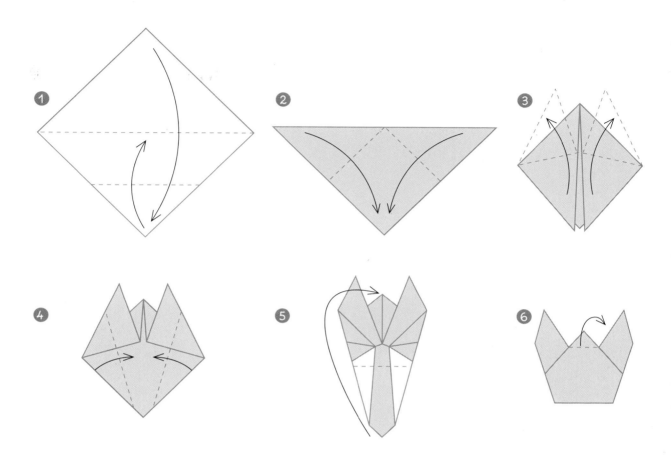

STEPS:

1. FOLD top corner of square paper down to bottom; REOPEN. FOLD bottom corner up to middle; REFOLD top down.

2. FOLD left and right corners down to bottom.

3. FOLD bottom points up, angled, beyond top edges. (Where you fold will determine length of ears; make some shorter than others if desired.)

4. FOLD sides in at an angle, as shown.

5. FOLD bottom point up to meet the top center point; FLIP over.

6. FOLD tips of center points to the back. DRAW on facial details.

PIPE CLEANER PALS

What could be better than hanging out with a barrel of monkeys, having a snack with a squirrel, or playing dress-up with a chameleon? Maybe you can't bring real wildlife home, but you can make do by making your own. These fuzzy animals come together with just a few coils, snips, and dots of glue.

squirrel This funny guy, like all the creatures on these pages, was formed by shaping a head and neck from one pipe cleaner, then wrapping a marker with a second pipe cleaner to make a coil and slipping it over the first to create the body. For features—ears, eyes, a bushy tail—attach snippets of other pipe cleaners or bits of felt with glue.

Can you spot the lizard in this picture? The chameleon's chief talent is blending into his surroundings. Craft him from green pipe cleaners and let him hide in plain sight—only his darting orange tongue and yellow felt eyes will give him away.

tiger Black stripes on orange fur give the tiger his distinctive look. Apply the stripes with permanent marker after twisting the big cat into shape with orange pipe cleaners.

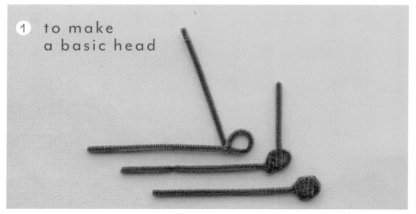

1. to make a basic head

2. to make a basic body

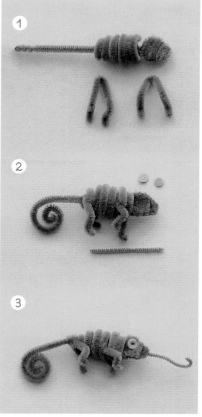

SUPPLIES:

- Pipe cleaners
- Marker (for shaping body and making details)
- Felt
- Scissors or nail clippers
- White craft glue

BASIC STEPS:

1. To make a basic head: MAKE a loop in the middle of a pipe cleaner. The size and shape of the loop determine the size and shape of the head. WRAP head from neck to nose (the remaining length will hold body in place and form tail).

2. To make a basic body: COIL pipe cleaner around a marker (the thicker the marker, the fatter the animal) and SLIDE off.

to make a chameleon

1. Make basic head and body shapes, leaving tail extra long for curling. SLIDE body into place. SLIP legs between coils, and twist to secure.

2. CUT out felt eyes; GLUE on. BEND legs at knees and feet. CUT a skinny pipe cleaner for tongue.

3. DRAW pupils on eyes with a permanent marker. SLIDE tongue into face; curl end.

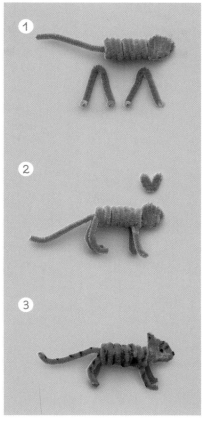

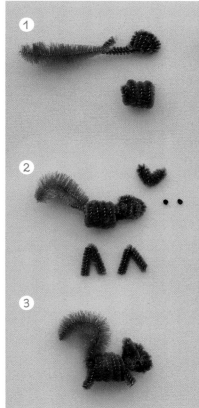

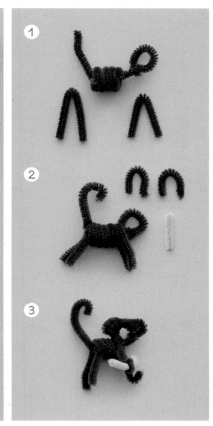

to make a tiger

1. Make basic head and body shapes. SLIDE body into place. SLIP back legs over tail; TWIST to secure. Slip front legs behind first coil and twist.

2. SLIDE ears through top of head, and reshape. BEND tip of tail.

3. CUT eyes and nose from felt; GLUE on. TRIM fur on face and ears with scissors. ADD stripes with marker.

to make a squirrel

1. Make basic head shape, leaving a shorter length on the end of the head piece for a hook. HOOK a piece of fluffy pipe cleaner onto it. MAKE a short body.

2. SLIDE body into place. Shape ears. SLIP through top of head. CUT felt eyes; GLUE on. PLACE legs over front and back coils, and TWIST to secure.

3. CURL tail.

to make a monkey

1. Make basic head shape, leaving face loop unwrapped. BEND tail up. FORM a short body, and SLIDE into place. SLIP long legs in front and back of the coils, and TWIST to secure.

2. TWIST ends of ears onto head. CURL tail. CUT a yellow piece for a banana.

3. CURL front paw around banana.

PAPER BAG PUPPETS

Turn paper lunch sacks upside down and glue on paper details to produce a gaggle of adorable animal puppets. Little hands can easily manipulate small bags—3-by-6-inch flat-bottom bags with side pleats are best—but you can use any size bag you have on hand. Brown lunch bags are ideal for dogs and lions; look for pink gift bags for the pigs. Craft a pair of "curtains" from poster board and decorative paper to make a theater for the puppet show, or just send the puppeteers behind the sofa for an impromptu performance.

HOW-TO

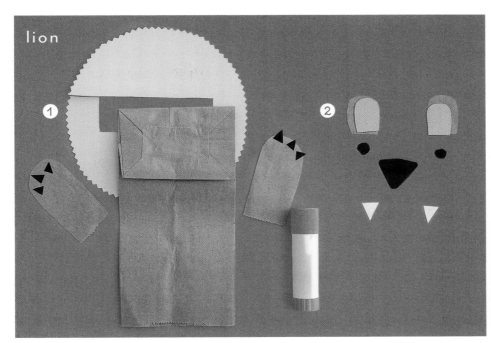

SUPPLIES:

· **Paper Bag Puppets templates** (see page 328)
· **Scissors**
· **Pinking shears**
· **Construction and decorative papers**
· **Flat-bottom paper bags**
· **White craft glue or glue stick**

tip ✳
Glue tiny details, such as claws, onto larger paper pieces before assembling the puppet.

to make a lion

1. Use template to CUT a large circle for the mane from yellow construction paper (use pinking shears around edge). CUT a rectangle out of the center, and SLIP the bag's bottom into the opening to create face; glue to secure.

2. Use templates to CUT ears and arms from another bag; CUT inner ears, eyes, nose, teeth, and claws from construction paper. GLUE on features (see tip above). ATTACH arms to front half of side pleats, ears and teeth under face.

to make a pig

1. GLUE pink construction paper to bottom of a pink gift bag to hide creases.

2. Use templates to CUT ears and snout from decorative paper in a rosy shade; glue in place. ADD tiny black construction-paper eyes and nostrils.

3. CUT arms from pink construction paper; GLUE to front half of the bag's side pleats.

to make a dog

1. FOLD under lower corners of bag's flattened bottom to shape face, and GLUE in place.

2. Use templates to CUT nose and belly from white construction paper, and ears and tail from brown. CUT eyes and nose from black paper, and tongue from pink.

3. GLUE everything in place, securing tongue under face and tail to the back of bag.

BALLOON ANIMALS

Clever twists or party tricks aren't needed to make a trio of lofty creatures. Just start with ordinary helium-filled balloons. Cut facial features and legs out of airy tissue paper, so the balloon stays aloft, and fashion ears out of lightweight paper that won't flop, such as vellum. Affix with double-sided tape (ears and legs should have folded tabs).

COTTON-BALL SHEEP

Real sheep are covered in fleece as white as snow, but you can make your own cuddly little lambs out of black paper and cotton balls.

SUPPLIES:

- Black card stock
- Colored pencil
- Scissors
- Hole punch
- String
- White craft glue
- Cotton balls

STEPS:

1. DRAW a sheep shape onto black card stock with pencil and CUT out.

2. PUNCH a hole at top, THREAD string through, and TIE ends together.

3. GLUE cotton balls to both sides, leaving the face and leg areas uncovered. HANG a small flock from a window or in a doorway.

ROCK FRIENDS

Those smooth stones you collect on nature walks and on strolls along the shore have a lot of life in them—you just need to apply some paint and glue to form alligators, ladybugs, frogs, and more. You can even paint a whole school of fish like the one shown at the beginning of the book.

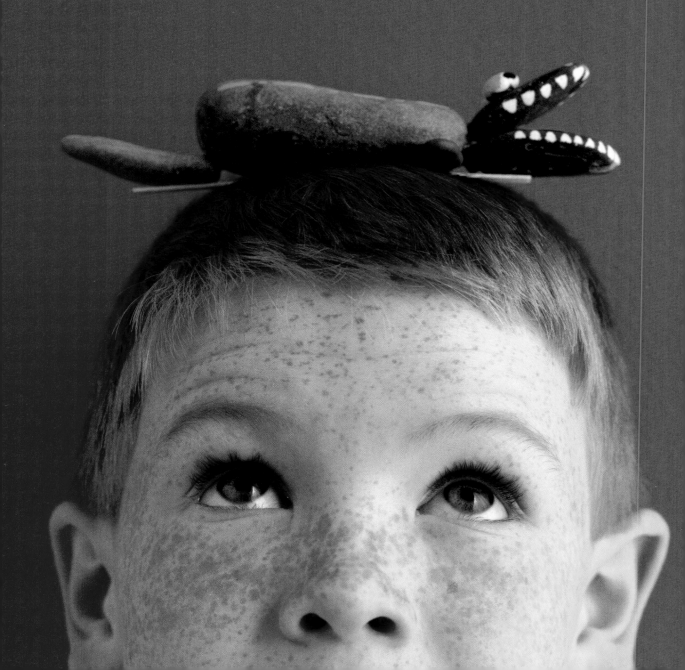

alligator This great gator is held together mostly with wooden coffee stirrers and glue; like his amphibian pals, he's made up of many parts. A simple scale design on his back and a set of sharp painted teeth bring him to life. Watch out for those chompers!

SUPPLIES:

- Paper and pencil to sketch
- Rocks
- Modeling clay
- Cement glue, such as 527
- Wooden coffee stirrers
- Scissors
- Acrylic paint and fine paintbrush

BASIC STEPS:

1. SKETCH your idea on paper. For creatures that require more than one rock, ARRANGE the rocks until the figure looks right. GLUE large body parts together; you can use modeling clay to support the pieces while the glue dries (putting the clay in the alligator's mouth, for example). For body parts that don't overlap each other a lot, GLUE lengths of wooden coffee stirrers underneath for more support.

2. GLUE on small stones for feet, eyes, and other details. When glue is dry, PAINT the sticks to match the stones, ADD paint to create features, and REMOVE clay.

ladybugs Creating a family of red-winged ladies couldn't be simpler: Each is made from a single rock. Sketch a pair of wings and dots for eyes on paper first, then re-create the look with paint on a series of oval stones, ranging in size from little to teensy-tiny.

turtle This little guy needs a bit of coaxing to come out of his shell. Paint a basic turtle-shell shape onto a big, round rock (here, thin green lines were painted as outlines and filled in with a lighter shade of green). Secure the smaller parts—four oval stones for feet, a skinny tail, an angled head—to the body with glue and coffee stirrers. Finish by painting on eyes and toenails.

frogs A pair of happy bullfrogs is marked by big, lazy eyes and tongues ready to catch passing flies. Glue two paddle-like feet under the round bodies, and tiny stones atop for the eyes. Paint dots in various sizes and shades of green.

CLOTHESPIN CHARACTERS

Fill a miniature farmyard with double-sided animals you draw yourself.
Stand them up on legs formed from ordinary clothespins.

SUPPLIES:

· White paper
· Markers or crayons
· Scissors
· Clothespins

STEPS:

1. FOLD white paper in half and DRAW an animal on one side, aligning its bottom with the fold.

2. CUT out (do not cut fold), and DRAW mirror image of animal on the other side.

3. For the legs, CLIP on 2 clothespins— use small ones for a squat creature, like a duck, and big ones for a cow.

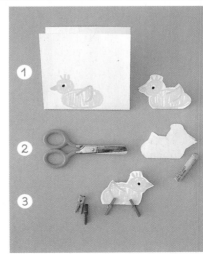

TWIG DOG

Try teaching this dog a new trick: how to "sit" on your finger. To make him, you'll need a small stick with a branch on either side. An adult should cut the stick so there's a half inch above and below the branches, then trim the branches to a few inches. Draw a friendly face on paper; cut it out and glue to the top of the stick. Try to balance the twig on your finger; keep trimming the branches until it stays in place.

EGGS-TRAORDINARY CREATURES

Here's a plan worth hatching: Use hollowed-out eggshells and a few crafts supplies to make a flock of bluebirds or a barnyard full of cows, pigs, and chickens. You can begin with white eggs and dye them as you like. Brown eggs are a natural starting point for animals with dark fur or feathers, and tiny speckled quail eggs are sized right for baby cows. Make them by the dozen!

bluebirds

These baby birds started out white. Dyed a light blue, then outfitted with crepe-paper wings and beaks, they're now singing for their supper. Arrange the little family in a nest of shredded kraft paper.

Let's mooove!

pigs This pale pink mama and her piglet are cooling off in a puddle of construction-paper mud. Their legs are made with pipe-cleaner snippets; their ears from crepe paper. For the nose, glue on a button. To make a curly tail, pull a plain piece of embroidery floss along scissors, as you would to curl a ribbon; glue in place.

cows An udderly adorable calf starts out as a speckled quail egg, and a pair of Holsteins gets their spots from black paint. The bull with the rounded furry legs is made from a smaller brown egg. All have crepe-paper features and embroidery-floss or yarn tails. Use a piece of pipe cleaner (add spots with a marker) for each pair of legs.

chickens This brood poses for a family portrait to welcome their latest addition. All the family members share fun features fashioned from felt and crepe paper—beaks, feet, and cockscomb feathers—but the chicks are dyed bright yellow.

SUPPLIES:

- Eggs
- Utility knife
- Paper clip
- Ear syringe
- Straight pins
- Foam board
- Paper towels
- Jar
- Vinegar
- Food coloring
- Paper cups
- Tongs
- Scissors
- Construction paper, pipe cleaners, felt, or crepe paper (for embellishments)
- White craft glue
- Pink buttons (for pigs)
- Clear tape
- Tempera paint and paintbrush or marker
- Embroidery floss or yarn

tip ✳

Make a board for drying the eggs evenly; place even rows of straight pins in a piece of foam board.

BASIC STEPS:

1. An adult should PIERCE each egg at both ends with a utility knife, widening one hole a bit.

2. Working over a bowl, POKE a straightened paper clip through wide hole in egg; stir yolk.

3. PLACE ear syringe in smaller hole; SQUEEZE. Contents will pour out of egg and into bowl. Repeat with remaining eggs. (Wash hands well before proceeding.)

to dye the eggs

1. COVER work area with paper towels. In a jar, MIX 1 teaspoon vinegar, 20 drops food coloring, and 1 cup warm water.

2. DUNK egg (weight it down with a paper cup filled halfway with water). SOAK 5 minutes for light colors, 10 minutes for darker shades.

3. REMOVE egg with tongs and let dry on prepared board.

to embellish the eggs

1. CUT out feet from felt or construction paper; or make legs by bending a pipe cleaner into a V shape. GLUE to egg so it can stand (use a fine paintbrush to apply small amounts of glue).

2. CUT out ears, horns, and combs from felt or crepe paper. GLUE to egg and let dry at least 20 minutes. For pigs, GLUE on button noses (use tape to secure them while they dry, then gently peel off).

3. ADD eyes and nostrils with paint or a marker. GLUE on embroidery-floss or yarn tails.

FELTED FINGER PUPPETS

Try this on for handfuls of fun: Assemble an entire zoo (or barnyard, or jungle) of fuzzy puppets, each sized just right for tiny fingers, using little more than felting wool, soap, and water. Use the creatures to put on a show or just tuck them into your pocket as on-the-go companions.

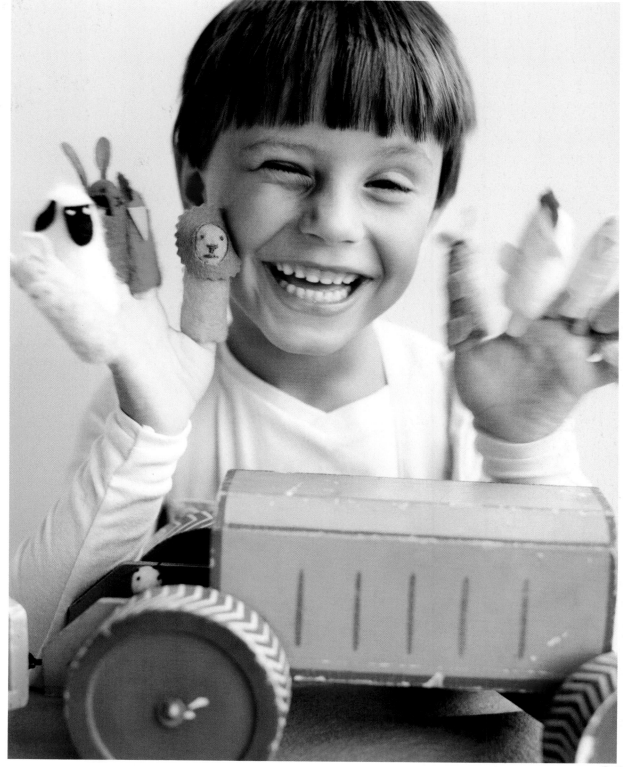

FELTED FINGER PUPPETS HOW-TO

SUPPLIES:

- Dye-free liquid dishwashing detergent
- Pitcher
- Wool roving (unspun wool); available at crafts stores
- Washboard
- Embroidery needle
- Embroidery floss
- Wool felt
- Scissors
- Felted Finger Puppets templates (see page 329)
- Fabric glue

BASIC STEPS:

1. MIX 4 tablespoons of liquid dishwashing detergent with 6 cups hot water in a pitcher. WRAP felting wool in layers around the pointer finger on the hand you don't write with. The wool should be snug but not tight. ADD wool until you can't feel your knuckles through it. (The soft wool should be about ⅛ inch thick when pressed.)

2. DIP your wool-wrapped finger in the hot soapy water, and PRESS with the fingertips of your other hand; continue to DIP and SQUEEZE until the fibers seem to hold together. Now you can ADD stripes (as for the bumblebee): WORK strips of a different color felting wool into the puppet with your fingertips.

3. STRENGTHEN the felt by rubbing it on the washboard. CHANGE directions as you RUB, and don't press very hard. RINSE under the faucet when done; remove from finger and LET dry completely before proceeding.

4. SEW eyes, antennae, and other tiny details directly onto dry puppet with embroidery floss, or onto store-bought felt for monkey, pig, and sheep.

5. Use templates to CUT ears, wings, and similar pieces from store-bought felt, enlarging or reducing them a bit if necessary. GLUE all features to puppet.

HAND-DRAWN STUFFED ANIMALS

Imagine if hand-drawn monsters, woodland creatures, and fairy-tale characters could jump right off the sketch pad. Follow these steps, and you can set your own artwork free. Little ones should ask a grown-up to sew their animals using their illustrations as a pattern. Older kids can go ahead and do the drawing, cutting, and sewing themselves. Don't worry about perfection—these playful characters are meant to be one of a kind.

I'm all stuffed up

STUFFED ANIMALS HOW-TO

SUPPLIES:

- Paper and colored
  pencils to sketch
- Scissors
- Pins
- Felt or other fabric
- Tailor's chalk
- Fabric scissors
- Needle and thread
- Buttons
- Polyester stuffing
- Pipe cleaners, yarn,
  ribbon, and other items
  for embellishments

BASIC STEPS:

1. SKETCH a character onto paper. Make a photocopy if you want to keep the original or make it smaller or larger. CUT out only the parts that will be stuffed; ears and limbs can be made from other material and sewn on later.

2. PIN pattern, facedown, to 2 pieces of fabric, which can be the same or different colors or material. TRACE pattern with tailor's chalk, leaving about ¼ inch of extra space all around; CUT out both layers. UNPIN pattern.

3. SEW the creature's features, such as button eyes, a felt mouth, or inner ears, to the front piece of fabric.

4. RE-PIN the 2 fabric pieces together with the features on the inside. SEW together with a needle and thread or a sewing machine, leaving an opening for stuffing.

5. TURN the pieces right side out. FILL with stuffing, then SEW closed.

6. FINISH by attaching ears, limbs, or other details. You can use felt, pipe cleaners, yarn, ribbon, or other things you might find around the house to complete your animal.

1

2

3

4

5

6

ears

arms

legs

POM-POM ANIMALS

These characters are easier to make than they look, thanks to a useful little tool called a pom-pom maker, available at crafts stores or online. Once you get the hang of winding and snipping and fluffing, you can put together a cuddly friend in no time.

o w l s Whooo goes there? Why it's a mama owl, made from a small pom-pom stitched atop a larger one, and her single-puffball baby.

bunnies Shy rabbits hop along a field of tall shredded-paper grass, looking for veggies to bring to their picnic. If you don't have a pom-pom maker small enough for a baby bunny, you can always make a larger pom-pom and trim it down to size.

POM-POM ANIMALS HOW-TO

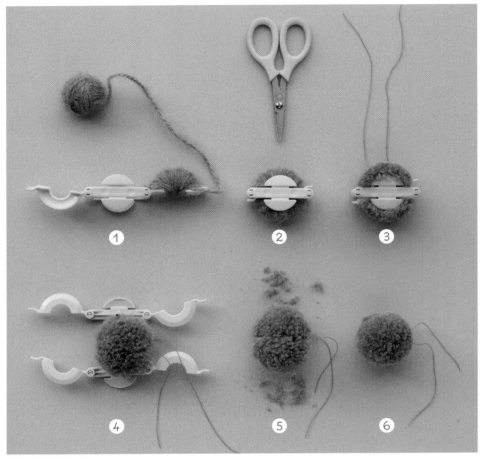

BASIC STEPS:

1. OPEN the two arms on top of a pom-pom maker and START winding yarn at one end; GO back and forth over the arms with the yarn until it is wrapped as densely as desired. CLOSE arms and OPEN the arms on the bottom; REPEAT wrapping.

2. Holding the pom-pom maker closed, use scissors to SNIP the yarn along the center of the rounded edges. Then CUT a length of matching embroidery floss and TIE the pom-pom in the center; pull tight and knot twice.

3. OPEN the pom-pom maker's arms, then carefully PULL the two sides of the maker apart and off the pom-pom.

4. TRIM any long or straggly yarn ends; if desired, TRIM the pom-pom further for a denser, smaller ball.

5. LEAVE the floss you tied off with intact if you plan to ATTACH the pom-pom to another one.

to make a bunny

1. MAKE two light brown pom-poms, one for the body and the other smaller, for the head.

2. STITCH the head to the body using a needle and the tail of the embroidery floss used to tie it (or attach with tacky glue).

3. Use the templates (page 329) to CUT out ears from tan felt; CUT tiny eyes and a nose from black felt. CUT whiskers from white waxed thread. GLUE in place.

POM-POM ANIMALS HOW-TO

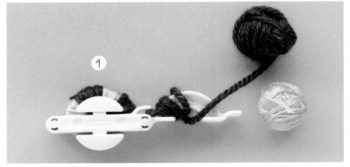

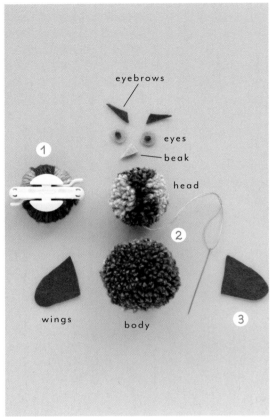

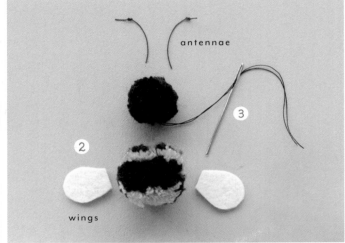

to make an owl

1. MAKE two pom-poms, a dark brown one for the body and a smaller, striped gray-and-brown one for the head (see tip, opposite, for how to make stripes).

2. STITCH the head to the body using a needle and the tail of the embroidery floss used to tie it (or ATTACH with tacky glue).

3. USE templates (page 329) to CUT out the owl's wings and facial features from felt. GLUE in place.

to make a bumblebee

1. MAKE two pom-poms, one striped with black and yellow (see tip, opposite), the other slightly smaller and solid black.

2. STITCH the head to the body using a needle and the tail of the embroidery floss used to tie it (or ATTACH with tacky glue).

3. USE templates to CUT a pair of wings from white felt. For antennae, CUT two lengths of waxed thread, and KNOT at one end. GLUE in place.

bumblebee The striped pom-pom of a handmade bumble is one piece crafted in alternating bunches of black and yellow. Felt wings and waxed-thread antennae complete his buzz-worthy suit.

SHELL MENAGERIE

The sea can inspire you to create animals of all sorts—and not just the kinds with fins, scales, and tentacles. You can glue seashells together to make land-loving creatures, too; collect a bunch and then experiment with shapes and sizes before gluing them in place. Sturdy bivalve shells make fine bodies and heads, while tall, skinny augers are perfect for legs and arms. If you can't collect them from the shore, inexpensive bags of shells can be found at crafts stores or gift shops.

funny faces
For a collection of characters, glue smaller shells (or craft beads) onto larger ones to make facial features like eyes, mouths, and noses.

turkeys These puffed-up turkeys shake their scallop-shell tail feathers and strut on olive-shell feet. Their bodies are made from still-connected mussels.

giraffe Pointy swirled shells, called *augers*, make up this giraffe's neck and legs. A Babylon shell is just the right shape for his round midsection.

poodle Tiny pink rice shells grace the ears of this well-groomed canine. Her coat is made from frilly ark shells, and she has prim cerith-shell legs.

koala The curvy shapes of clam and scallop shells are just right for koala bodies, ears, feet, and noses. Choose larger shells for a papa bear, smaller ones for a joey. A couple of tall, slim razor clam shells become eucalyptus trees, with cockles for leaves.

SHELL MENAGERIE HOW-TO

SUPPLIES:

- Shells in various shapes and sizes
- Cement glue, such as 527
- Modeling clay
- Beads
- Small paintbrush

BASIC STEPS:

1. Form the body: LAY a clamshell down lengthwise and GLUE shells to the bottom edge for feet (we used 2 smaller bivalves for the koala). Use modeling clay to SUPPORT shells while the glue dries.

2. For the face, GLUE small shells for ears and a nose onto the front of a medium-size clamshell; GLUE tiny beads in place for eyes (a small paintbrush is helpful for dotting on the glue). TUCK clay underneath for support while drying.

3. When the glue is completely dry, JOIN the 2 body parts and SUPPORT with clay until glue sets. (Modify these techniques to make other animals.)

CANDY MONSTERS

Come October, nearly everything takes on new, frightful personalities—even candies can get into the act. Sticks of hard candy, marshmallows, licorice whips, gumdrops, and tiny sprinkles can be used to create a variety of ghouls and goblins, from a toothy skeleton to a hulking goon hatched straight from a mad scientist's lab.

wrap it up

After you assemble your beastly crew, wrap each character in cellophane and secure with a length of ribbon. They make great treats to fend off tricksters on All Hallows Eve.

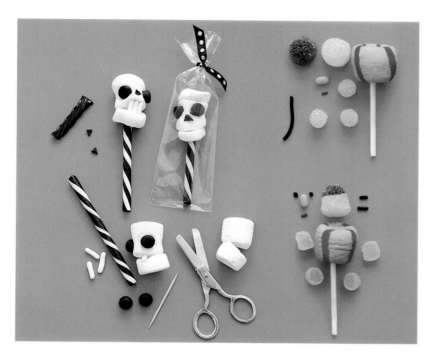

SUPPLIES:

- Scissors
- Marshmallows (for skull)
- Toothpick
- White candy-coated licorice pastels
- Black licorice drops, laces, and twists
- Candy sticks
- Gumdrops
- Large lollipops
- Candy-coated mints
- Candy sprinkles

to make a skull pop

1. With scissors, CUT 1 white marshmallow to make pieces for head and jaw, exposing stickiness.

2. POKE holes into marshmallow pieces with a toothpick to make sticky spots for eyes, teeth, and nose. Poke white licorice pastels into jaw for teeth, and PRESS black licorice drops into head for eyes. SNIP a piece of black licorice twist into a small triangle for the nose, and PRESS into place.

3. POKE a few times into marshmallow with the toothpick to make a large hole for a candy stick. PUSH candy stick into hole, through jaw, and into skull.

to make monster pops

1. CUT top and bottom off white gumdrop and CUT top off black gumdrop. STICK black gumdrop to top of white gumdrop for head. STICK onto lollipop. CUT a smaller spice drop in half lengthwise for arms, and CUT tops off 2 more to use for legs; PRESS into place.

2. POKE holes with a toothpick and ADD tiny candy details, such as a candy-coated mint nose, and snipped licorice or sprinkle eyes, neck bolts, and mouth. (Make green monster following same directions.)

PUMPKIN KITTEN

Whether you're a Halloween witch in need of a loyal companion or a black cat looking for a kitty to cuddle, this palm-size feline is up to the task. Simply connect two pumpkins—one small, the other even tinier—with skewers, then add paper ears, whiskers, and other details.

frisky friend
This fun and easy pumpkin project requires minimal carving; an adult should take charge of cutting out the eyes and the top of the smaller pumpkin. The rest is simple assembly and can be completed by children of all ages.

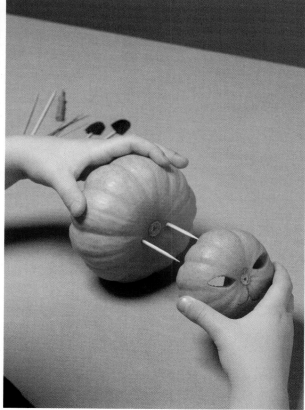

SUPPLIES:

· 2 small pumpkins in graduated sizes
· Pumpkin saw
· Melon baller
· Wax pencil
· 2 wooden skewers
· Scissors
· Black construction paper
· Tape
· Toothpicks
· Waxed twine
· Broom bristles

STEPS:

1. CUT top off smaller pumpkin with a pumpkin saw, and HOLLOW out the insides with a melon baller. Keep stem on larger pumpkin intact for a tail.

2. DRAW features on smaller pumpkin with wax pencil (indentation on bottom will be the nose). CUT out eyes with pumpkin saw and ETCH curved slits for cat's mouth.

3. DECIDE where head will be positioned. JOIN head to body using 2 wooden skewers.

4. Using scissors, CUT ears from construction paper; TAPE to toothpicks and insert in place. TUCK waxed twine inside etched slits for cat's mouth. For whiskers, PIERCE holes with skewer; INSERT broom bristles.

MERINGUE MICE

Eeeek! Was that a mouse? Never fear, these skittering critters are made of sweet meringue. With black licorice tails and perky sliced-almond ears, they're almost too cute to trap—or to eat.

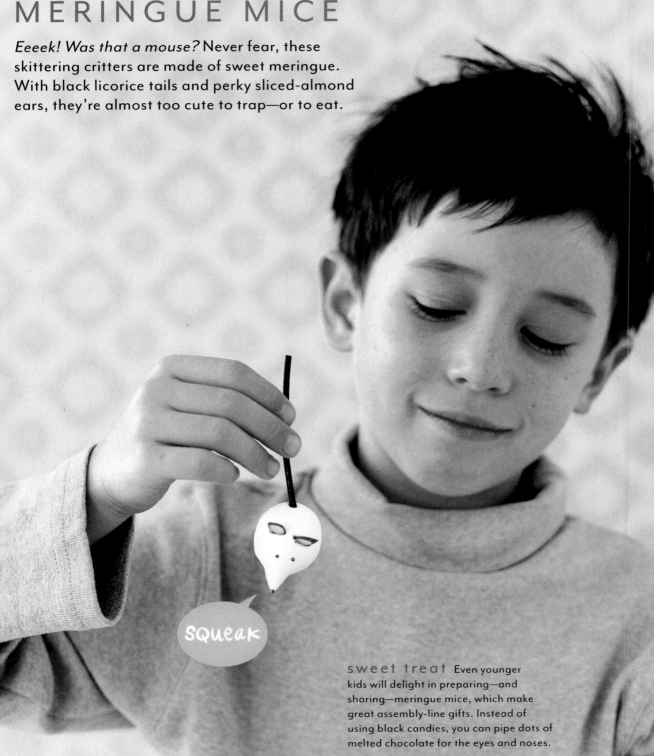

squeak

sweet treat Even younger kids will delight in preparing—and sharing—meringue mice, which make great assembly-line gifts. Instead of using black candies, you can pipe dots of melted chocolate for the eyes and noses.

MERINGUE MICE HOW-TO

to make the meringue

INGREDIENTS:

- 2 large egg whites, room temperature
- ½ cup sugar
- Pinch of cream of tartar
- ¼ teaspoon pure vanilla extract

DIRECTIONS:

1. *Combine the egg whites, sugar, and cream of tartar in the heat-proof bowl of an electric mixer, and place it over a pan of simmering water. Whisk constantly until whites are warm to the touch and sugar is dissolved, about 2 minutes. Test by rubbing the mixture between your fingers; it should be completely smooth, not grainy.*

2. *Transfer bowl to mixer stand; fit mixer with the whisk attachment. Starting on low speed and gradually increasing to high, beat egg-white mixture until completely cool and stiff, glossy peaks form, about 10 minutes. Add vanilla, and mix until combined.*

MAKES ENOUGH FOR ABOUT 50 MICE

SUPPLIES:

- Meringue recipe and ingredients (see below)
- Pastry bag fitted with a large round tip (such as Ateco 803)
- 2 baking sheets lined with parchment paper
- Black licorice laces, cut into 3-inch lengths
- Tweezers
- Black nonpareil candies
- Sliced almonds
- Wire rack

STEPS:

1. PLACE meringue in a pastry bag fitted with the large round tip. PIPE teardrop shapes of meringue about 2 inches apart onto parchment-lined baking sheets: First HOLD the tip close to the parchment and SQUEEZE a 1-inch-diameter oval mound; then REDUCE pressure and LIFT the tip up and slightly to one side to form a pointed end for the nose.

2. After all the meringue is piped, ADD licorice-lace tails, and then use tweezers to ADD tiny nonpareil candies for their eyes and noses. PLACE sliced-almond ears last, so they don't get bumped out of position.

3. PREHEAT oven to 175°F, with racks in upper and lower thirds. BAKE meringue mice until they are hard when gently tapped but still white, about 1½ hours. (Do not overbake, or they will crack and begin to brown.) TRANSFER to a wire rack and let cool completely. STORE in an airtight container at room temperature for up to 1 week.

FELT MICE

Not a creature was stirring, not even . . . Well, maybe there *is* a mouse or two running around this holiday season. But these are so sweet, cut from felt and finished with striped-candy tails, no one will mind. Hand one out to everyone on your gift list.

SUPPLIES:

- Felt Mice templates (see page 329)
- Scissors
- Felt in various colors
- White craft glue
- Wrapped candy canes

STEPS:

1. Use templates to CUT out body and ears from felt in the same color. CUT inner ears and a dot for a nose from felt in a contrasting color. CUT tiny dots for eyes from black.

2. GLUE the face and inner ears in place. MAKE slits in body for ears and tail where marked.

3. SLIP ears through slits at front; SLIDE a candy cane through body slits, tucking the end underneath.

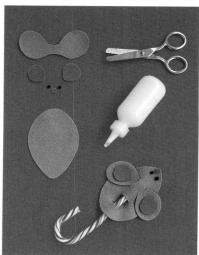

PINECONE PENGUINS

Pinecones abound in the chilly months—take a walk through the yard or the woods and in no time you'll have an armload. Why not use them for creating a colony of frosty, feathered birds? For wings, tails, and ears, peel scales from big cones like those from eastern white, western white, and sugar pine trees.

there's snow place like home

north pole

frosty scene Penguins can't migrate far from their natural habitat, so use a mirror, extra pinecones, glitter, and some faux snow to make a frozen pond. The snowcapped mountain is made with card stock cut into an icicle pattern, glittered, then wrapped around a birch log and covered with cotton batting and faux snow.

SUPPLIES:

- Scissors
- 2 large pinecone scales (for wings)
- Sandpaper
- 1 small piece cut from top of a pinecone (for neck)
- White craft glue
- 1 long pinecone (for body)
- Small paintbrushes
- White acrylic paint
- White coarse glitter
- 1 acorn cap (for face)
- Brown acrylic paint

STEPS:

1. CUT the large pinecone scales so that each comes to a point, for wings.

2. SAND neck piece so it will fit easily onto top of pinecone body. BRUSH top of body with glue; ATTACH neck.

3. PAINT belly (cover scales completely) and half of acorn cap white (leave stem unpainted, for nose). Let dry completely.

4. BRUSH belly with glue; SPRINKLE with glitter. Let dry.

5. BRUSH neck with glue; ATTACH acorn-cap face, with painted portion on bottom. Let dry.

6. DOT brown paint onto face, for eyes.

7. BRUSH rounded end of each wing with glue, and ATTACH to body. Let dry.

ELFIN FAMILY

The North Pole—or any other wintry destination—is within easy reach when you re-create this charming tabletop scene. A family of elves gathers on a snowy hillside along with a tiny reindeer friend. Add artificial snow and a few bigger pinecones as trees in the background. For elves just like these, use cones from eastern white pine trees.

bearded elf **girl elf** **boy elf** **reindeer**

SUPPLIES:

- Colored and metallic pipe cleaners
- Scissors or nail clippers
- White and green bump chenille stems
- Tweezers
- Small paintbrush
- White craft glue
- Black seed beads
- Wooden craft beads (for heads)
- 2 small pinecone tops
- Acorn cap
- 4 scales of longleaf pinecone (for reindeer legs)
- Small pinecones
- Fine glitter (optional)

STEPS:

1. SHAPE short lengths of pipe cleaners into arms, legs, and hair for the girl. Make antlers by twisting short pieces around middle of longer pieces. CUT a strip of white chenille stem for the elf's beard.

2. Using tweezers and a paintbrush, GLUE black seed beads to wooden craft beads to form eyes and mouths for the elves; GLUE slightly larger seed beads to a pinecone top for the reindeer's head.

3. For the bearded elf's hat, COIL red metallic pipe cleaner into a cone by wrapping it around your little finger. GLUE hat and beard to wooden-bead face.

4. For the girl, boy, and reindeer, GLUE hair, hats (pinecone top for girl, acorn cap for boy), and antlers in place.

5. Working from back to front, PUSH pipe-cleaner arms and legs into the pinecones to secure; GLUE scales in place for reindeer legs.

6. GLUE the heads to the pinecone bodies; let dry. To glitter pinecones (if desired), HOLD a cone carefully, and brush craft glue over tips of scales. Then, holding the cone over a bowl, SPOON fine glitter over scales. Let dry.

RICE-CEREAL CRITTERS

Crisped-rice treats may have a reputation for being square, but with a little creativity and some edible embellishments, these lunch-box favorites can become the life of any party. Start with the ladybugs, bumble bees, and caterpillars shown here, then use other colorful trimmings (opposite) to create other cute creatures.

tip ✳
Make shapes one at a time, working quickly while cereal mixture is soft and sticky.

INGREDIENTS:

- 5 tablespoons unsalted butter, cut into pieces
- 6 cups mini marshmallows
- 8 cups puffed-rice cereal, such as Rice Krispies
- Vegetable oil cooking spray

DIRECTIONS:

1. *Melt butter over low heat in a large saucepan. Add marshmallows and cook, stirring occasionally with a wooden spoon, until melted, about 10 minutes.*

2. *Remove from heat and stir in cereal until evenly combined. Coat a large bowl with cooking spray. Spoon cereal mixture into bowl and cover with plastic wrap so it won't harden.*

MAKES ENOUGH FOR ABOUT 70 CRITTERS

SUPPLIES:

- Cereal Mixture recipe and ingredients (see above)
- Butter, for hands
- Scissors
- Black licorice laces
- Paring knife
- Gumdrops in red and yellow
- Wooden skewer or toothpick
- Candy wafers
- Green twizzle sticks

STEPS:

1. For each ladybug, ROLL cereal mixture with buttered hands into a 1-inch ball for the body. SNIP licorice into 2 tiny pieces for "eyes" and slightly larger pieces for dots; SNIP a 1-inch piece for a stripe. For the head, SLICE off one side of a red gumdrop to expose stickiness, then PRESS to the body. POKE holes in gumdrop and body with a skewer, then INSERT licorice pieces.

2. For each bumblebee, FOLLOW directions for ladybug (above), using a yellow gumdrop for the head and snipping licorice into antenna and 2 stripes along with the eyes. For wings, CUT slits in either side of the body with a knife, then INSERT a candy wafer into each.

3. For each caterpillar, ROLL cereal mixture into four or five ¾-inch balls and PRESS together to form the head and body. POKE holes into head and INSERT black licorice eyes and green twizzle stick antennae.

BUILD A LITTLE WORLD

A snowy urban landscape, a fully equipped auto body repair shop, a schoolhouse where you can make all the rules: If you can dream it up, you can build it.

SNOW GLOBES

A glittering snowfall makes any city sight—
traffic and taxicabs, historic landmarks and
high-rise buildings—look all the more magical.
Shape your own from bakeable clay and glue
them inside a homemade snow globe for an
instant wintry wonderland.

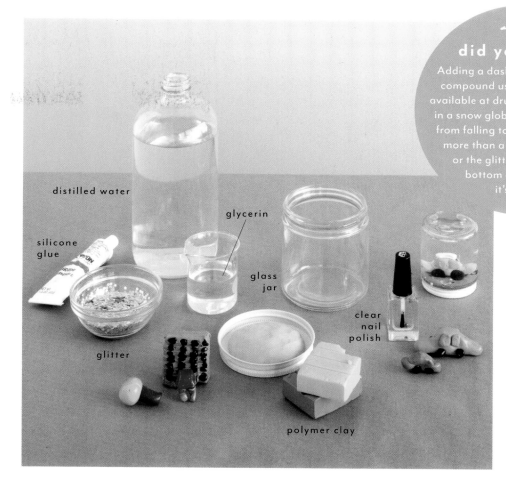

distilled water

glycerin

silicone glue

glass jar

glitter

clear nail polish

polymer clay

did you know?

Adding a dash of glycerin—a clear compound used in soap-making, available at drugstores—to the water in a snow globe will keep the glitter from falling too quickly. Don't add more than a few drops, though, or the glitter will stick to the bottom of the jar when it's flipped.

SUPPLIES:

· Sandpaper
· Glass jars with lids
· Polymer clay
· Clear nail polish
· Silicone glue
· Distilled water
· Glitter
· Glycerin

STEPS:

1. SAND the inside of jar lids until the surface is rough, so glue will adhere to it.

2. MOLD cars or buildings using polymer clay. BAKE according to clay manufacturer's instructions. LET cool completely, then COAT with nail polish to seal. Let dry. Adhere sculpture to inside of jar lid with silicone glue; let dry.

3. FILL the jar almost to the top with distilled water. Do not use tap water, as it can turn yellow over time. (Boiling does not remove impurities, either.) ADD a pinch of glitter and a few drops of glycerin.

4. APPLY a ring of glue to the mouth of the jar. Carefully SCREW on the lid tightly and let glue dry before turning jar over.

STICKVILLE

In this charming country getaway, wooden craft sticks stand in for logs and boards in a rustic cabin, fence, farm truck, and, naturally, an old-fashioned ice-pop stand.

pop-up shop
Every small town deserves a sweet spot. Label the signs using tiny rubber stamps or colored markers.

POP'S
FAMOUS
ICE
POPS

TODAY'S FLAVORS
orange
cherry
lemon
lime
grape

home sweet home Animals roam free at this cottage in the mountains. Let yours loose once the glue has completely dried on the house.

STICKVILLE HOW-TO

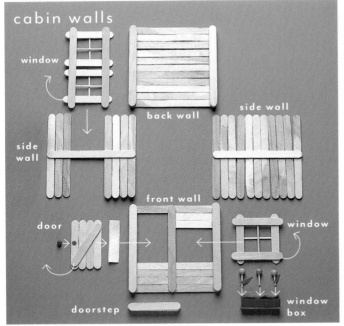

cabin walls

window

side wall

back wall

side wall

door

front wall

doorstep

window

window box

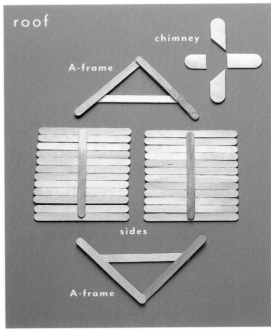

roof

chimney

A-frame

sides

A-frame

to make a basic structure

1. Modify these steps to design your own cabin. For walls, PLACE sticks side by side; leave gaps or use half-sticks to make space for windows and doors. On two opposing walls (shown top and bottom), JOIN sticks by gluing support sticks along ends; these provide a surface for gluing to adjacent walls. GLUE center supports on remaining walls and where you will have windows.

2. For the windows, GLUE together half-sticks and whole sticks; CREATE panes with toothpicks.

3. For the door, set out half-sticks; GLUE on a diagonal support stick and bead doorknob. For the doorstep, GLUE stacked half-sticks together.

4. For the window box, ATTACH one cut-off stick perpendicular to another (add clay inside; flowers are beads and paper leaves on cut-off toothpicks). Flip walls over and GLUE windows and window box to walls. For hinge, GLUE ribbon to door and doorframe. When all pieces are assembled, GLUE walls together.

to make a roof

1. LAY out 2 rows of sticks, each as wide as the house; GLUE on center supports. GLUE together 2 A-frames.

2. For the chimney, CUT 2 wide craft sticks into shapes as shown; GLUE together at sides.

3. GLUE edge of one roof side to the flat side of one A-frame; GLUE other roof side to same frame. GLUE on second A-frame. GLUE chimney. PLACE roof on house; SECURE with glue.

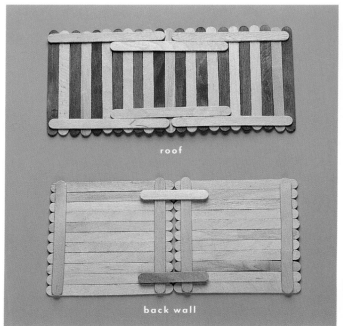

roof

back wall

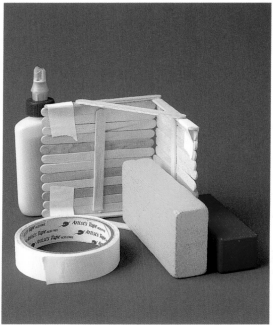

SUPPLIES:

- Plain and red craft sticks in whole, half, and wide sizes
- Wood glue
- Toothpicks
- Colorful beads
- Modeling clay
- Construction paper, for leaves
- Ribbon
- Masking tape, wooden blocks, and clothespins, for supports while drying
- Twine

to make an ice-pop stand

1. Modify the steps for a basic structure (opposite), making it extra wide and adding extra support sticks: CREATE a wide back wall and roof as shown above. Use red craft sticks for a striped roof. Make a wide, short front wall. GLUE the pieces together.

2. For a flavor list, TRIM craft sticks and glue them to twine to join them.

tips for assembly

All of these projects require wood glue. Allow 15 to 30 minutes of drying time before handling the glued parts. To make sure everything stays in place while drying, try the tips below:

- Prop up pieces that are glued at an angle, such as the roof, with light-colored modeling clay (it won't stain the sticks), molding it so it fits the areas that need support.

- Use masking tape to secure pieces, and wooden blocks to hold up adjacent walls and roof parts.

- Clamp flat pieces together with clothespins to help them bond better. This trick is especially useful for gluing on support sticks, such as on a long roof.

keep on truckin' A milk carton is used to form the body of this hardworking farm truck. Axle sticks are piled high to allow the carton to clear the wooden spool wheels.

STICKVILLE HOW-TO

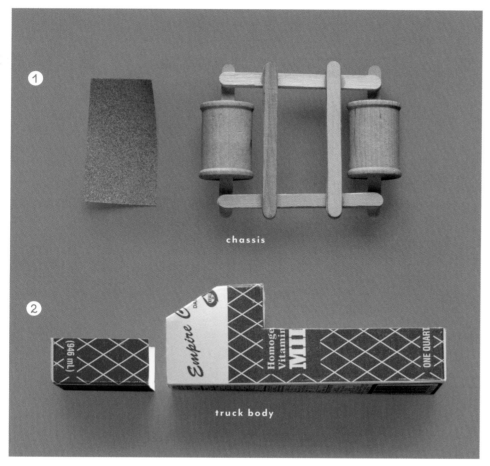

chassis

truck body

SUPPLIES:
- Craft sticks
- Wooden spools
- Sandpaper (if needed)
- Wood glue
- Milk carton
- Utility knife

to make a farm truck

1. For the wheels, SLIDE a craft stick into each wooden spool wheel (if needed, sand down sticks' sides so wheels can turn). To join wheels, GLUE 2 stacks of sticks to axles. Then ADD crossbeams by gluing more stacks between wheels until chassis (or support frame) is high enough for cab to clear wheels.

2. For cab, have an adult CUT off top of milk carton with a utility knife. FOLD one side of open carton straight in to make a windshield; the sides will fold in at an angle. CUT out a section from bottom of carton to make the truck bed; SLIDE piece from bottom into cab front. For truck bed's sides, GLUE sticks to inside of carton in a grid shape. GLUE truck body to chassis.

HORSE STABLE DIORAMA

Building a diorama—a miniature three-dimensional scene scaled to fit inside a frame—is a delight for any young crafter. This project involves outfitting a horse stable from a wood crate and is meant to be kept on display; tiny touches like soda-can-tab horseshoes and string bridles create a realistic scene.

HOW-TO

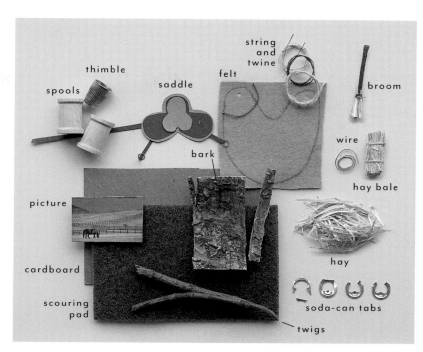

Labels on image: thimble, spools, saddle, felt, string and twine, broom, wire, hay bale, bark, picture, cardboard, scouring pad, hay, soda-can tabs, twigs

SUPPLIES:

- Wooden crate or box
- Scissors
- Cardboard
- Glue or hot-glue gun and glue stick
- Scouring pads
- Bark, twigs, and sticks
- Utility scissors
- Soda-can tabs
- Hay or grass
- String, wire, and twine
- Colored construction paper (for ribbons and saddle)
- Picture (for window)
- Wooden spools
- Marker
- Felt in various colors
- Horse Stable Diorama templates (see page 329)
- Plastic horses
- Thimble (for water bucket)
- Map tacks
- Jewelry jump rings

to make a stable

1. STAND crate on its side. Cut cardboard to desired size for floor. GLUE scouring pads to cardboard. Use scissors to CUT bark into fence rails and twigs into posts; glue together.

2. With utility scissors, CLIP soda-can tabs into horseshoes (an adult should do this). For hay bales, WRAP hay or grass with wire; cover wire with twine. Make broom out of twig, hay, and wire. SNIP out prize ribbons from colored paper, and CUT OUT a "window" from a magazine or download and print an image. COIL twine into "ropes." LABEL spools with marker (ours say OAT and GRAIN); CUT felt rounds to cover tops. STICK twigs together with glue to make shelves.

3. DRAW U shapes on felt for horse blankets, and CUT out; make saddle (right). For bridles, TIE string around horses' heads.

4. ARRANGE accessories (including thimble) in crate, then GLUE in place. Use map tacks to hang ropes. GLUE stick post in center; ATTACH bark stall divider.

to make a saddle

1. Use the template to CUT saddle layers from brown and tan construction paper or felt; GLUE layers together.

2. CUT 2 short thin strips for stirrups and 1 long strip for girth. FOLD one end of each stirrup through a jewelry jump ring, and glue. GLUE stirrups to saddle. WRAP girth around horse's belly; GLUE ends under saddle.

TOY BOATS

Anchors aweigh! If you long for a life on the water, you can build yourself
a boat—or a whole fleet of them—and play captain. The instructions
on page 82 are for making the sailboat; the same technique can be adapted
for any of the vessels on these pages. If you are combining many blocks,
tape them together first and try a test float to make sure your design
works. If your boat is tippy, use a bigger keel on the bottom to steady it.

✳ did you know?

Whether you have one sail or six, the boat works the same way: The keel beneath the water's surface holds everything steady. The longer or taller the boat, the bigger the keel should be. Test your boat in a bathtub or sink, then move on to the bigger waters of a nearby pond or lake if you're feeling adventurous. And don't forget to practice your captain's lingo. *Hoist the mainsail! Come about. Land ho!*

TOY BOAT HOW-TO

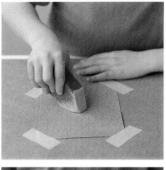

SUPPLIES:

- Clamp
- Wood blocks
- Saw
- Chopstick
- Drill
- Sandpaper
- Masking tape
- Wood glue
- Nontoxic water-based paint and paintbrush
- Polyurethane
- Tyvek envelope (such as an overnight mail envelope)
- Scissors
- Markers or stickers
- Hole punch
- Waxed twine
- Toy Boat templates (for clipper ship, see page 330)
- Toothpicks

BASIC STEPS:

1. These instructions are for making the sailboat shown on page 81, lower left; adapt the steps to make any of the other boats pictured. An adult should do this step: CLAMP a block to a worktable and saw off 2 corners to form the pointed bow. Set aside one corner scrap to use as a keel. SAW a chopstick to mast length. USE a very small drill bit to make 2 or 3 holes in the chopstick for attaching the sail. With a bigger bit, DRILL a hole in the top center of the boat (not all the way through) to hold the mast. TAPE down a piece of sandpaper and rub the block back and forth on it, to smooth the rough edges. Also SAND the keel.

2. If the boat body has multiple parts, GLUE them together first. Then GLUE the keel to the bottom and the mast into the top hole. WIPE off all excess glue and LET dry completely.

3. PAINT 2 or 3 coats, letting the paint dry between coats. PAINT on decorations such as racing stripes, portholes, and a carefully chosen name. Working in a well-ventilated room, an adult should SEAL the boat with 2 or 3 coats of polyurethane (drying between coats) to make her seaworthy.

4. For a sail, CUT a triangle out of a Tyvek envelope with the fold along the long side for strength. DECORATE with markers or stickers. PUNCH 2 or 3 holes along the side, and TIE the sail to the mast with waxed twine.

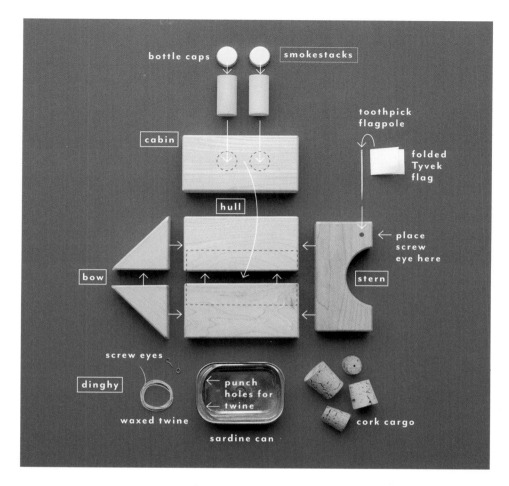

to make a tugboat (shown on page 81, lower right)

1. Following basic steps (opposite), GLUE two rectangular blocks side by side to form the hull, as shown in the diagram above, then ATTACH two triangle blocks to one end for the bow and a curved block to the other end for the stern. ATTACH another rectangular block to center of hull for the cabin.

2. GLUE bottle caps onto wooden cylinders for smokestacks and attach these to the cabin as shown. For the flagpole, GLUE a folded piece of Tyvek to a toothpick; TWIST a screw eye into top of stern. INSERT toothpick into screw eye.

3. TWIST a screw eye into center of stern's curve. For the dinghy, have an adult PUNCH holes into one end of a clean sardine can, then RUN twine through holes and CONNECT to the screw eye on the boat. FILL the can with cork cargo.

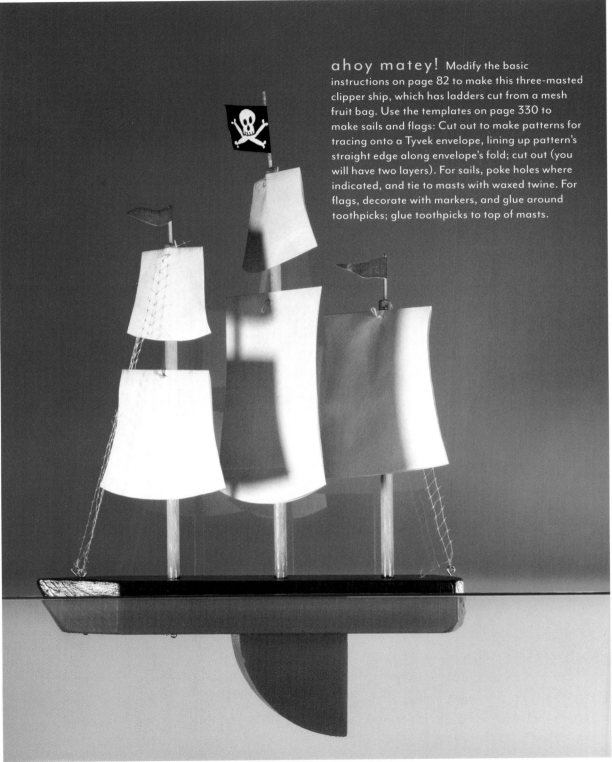

ahoy matey! Modify the basic instructions on page 82 to make this three-masted clipper ship, which has ladders cut from a mesh fruit bag. Use the templates on page 330 to make sails and flags: Cut out to make patterns for tracing onto a Tyvek envelope, lining up pattern's straight edge along envelope's fold; cut out (you will have two layers). For sails, poke holes where indicated, and tie to masts with waxed twine. For flags, decorate with markers, and glue around toothpicks; glue toothpicks to top of masts.

TOY BOAT HOW-TO

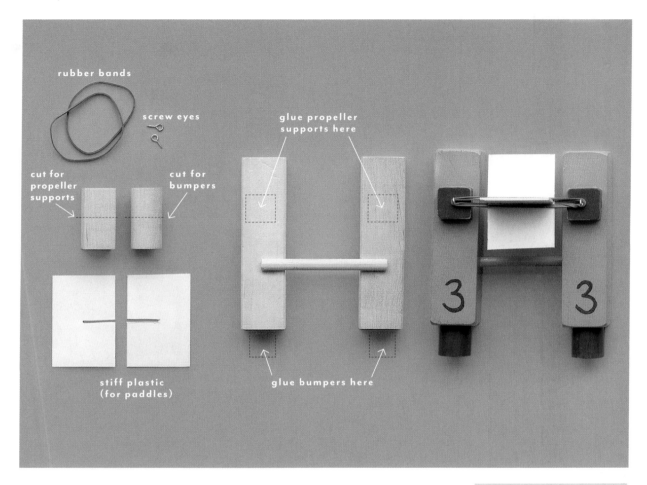

rubber bands

screw eyes

glue propeller supports here

cut for propeller supports

cut for bumpers

glue bumpers here

stiff plastic (for paddles)

to make a motorboat (shown on page 81, upper right)

1. USE long wood blocks to form a pontoon (flat-bottomed hull) and JOIN them together with a dowel; an adult should DRILL holes in the blocks' sides to fit the dowel. GLUE to secure.

2. CUT bumpers and propeller supports as shown; GLUE to pontoon. PAINT and seal the boat. ATTACH screw eyes in propeller supports.

3. For paddles, use stiff plastic (like the side of a plastic bottle) or balsa wood. CUT 2 rectangles with slits; SLIDE together at slits. LOOP rubber bands around the axis of the paddle, and PULL ends around screw eyes to attach pontoon.

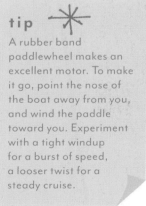

tip

A rubber band paddlewheel makes an excellent motor. To make it go, point the nose of the boat away from you, and wind the paddle toward you. Experiment with a tight windup for a burst of speed, a looser twist for a steady cruise.

FILE FOLDER VILLAGE

Turned on its side, a simple folder from any office-supply store looks just like a rooftop. With some helpful templates and a few folds and cuts, you can make a whole village worth of colorful houses in a forest of trees.

SUPPLIES:

· Pencil
· File Folder Village templates (see page 330)
· File folders
· Scissors
· Double-sided tape

STEPS:

1. TRACE house and tree templates onto file folders, lining up the center of the roof on the folder's existing fold, and CUT out.

2. To make a house, lightly SCORE walls on dotted lines (as indicated on template) and fold. TUCK the shaded tab behind the other end; SECURE with double-sided tape. LAY a strip of the tape along top edges of house; SET roof on, pressing gently.

3. For tree, CUT slits in the center as marked on the template. SLIP trees together at slits to interlock.

HOUSE OF CARDS

Making a house of cards that stays in place has never been so easy. Cut drinking straws into 2-inch segments. Make a ½-inch slit on each end of each straw. Cut 4-by-6-inch cards from cereal or sugar boxes, or other lightweight cardboard pieces. Create walls by attaching straws to the edges of the cards and connecting them to other cards. Fold cards in half to create corners.

TOY SERVICE STATION

Drivers, start your engines: Budding car enthusiasts will be busy for hours putting together this one-stop-shop for toy cars—complete with gas pumps, a car wash, and a full-service mechanic's shop. You can build the basic structure out of pieces of cardboard boxes; to make the machines and gadgets, you'll need to scavenge household objects from the kitchen, garage, and crafts closet.

tip

Stickers, stamps, and letter magnets work well for signs. Decorate walls and machines with construction paper or paint. Mark parking spaces with yellow electrical tape. Sandpaper looks like tarmac, and spools resemble oil drums. An oatmeal canister and bottle brushes become a toy-size car wash.

oatmeal container

aluminum pan

corrugated cardboard

hot-glue gun and glue stick

stickers

00 111
33 344
666 677
9999 $$

scissors

baby-bottle brushes

cleaning cloth

paper tube

tall straws

utility knife

matchbox

spice can

paintbrush

all-purpose glue

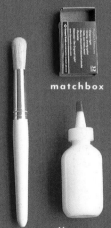

thread spools

acrylic paint

black and brown sandpaper

paper fasteners

electrical tape

letter magnets

rubber stamps

coffee-can lid

SERVICE STATION HOW-TO

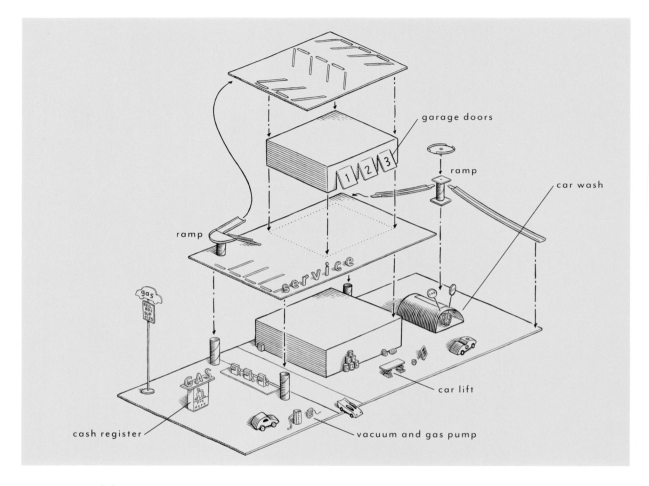

garage doors

ramp

car wash

ramp

service

car lift

gas

GAS

cash register

vacuum and gas pump

to assemble garage

1. Following the diagram, GLUE cardboard pieces in various sizes together, using paper-towel tubes as support columns for each floor.

2. To make garage doors, have an adult CUT flaps in one side of a cardboard box with a utility knife.

3. To attach a ramp, SLIDE the tab of a piece of a toy race track into the corrugated center of a cardboard platform. CUT off the lip on opposite sides of a coffee lid for a spinning turnaround. POKE a hole through the lid and a cardboard square; JOIN with a paper fastener and GLUE square to top of a paper-towel tube.

4. For the car lift, GLUE two accordion-folded strips of cardboard to a flat strip, adjusting folds until the lift stands upright.

5. For the cash register, DRAW an attendant on paper, and GLUE to a metal spice container.

6. Have an adult ATTACH letter magnets to cardboard with a hot-glue gun.

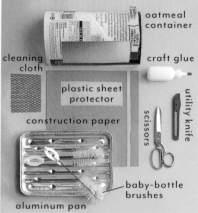

oatmeal container

craft glue

cleaning cloth

plastic sheet protector

utility knife

construction paper

scissors

aluminum pan

baby-bottle brushes

to make car wash

1. CUT off bottom and one side of an oatmeal carton. An adult should CUT out a skylight with a utility knife. CUT out a piece of plastic sheet protector slightly larger than skylight and GLUE in place.

2. MAKE 2 flaps on either side of carton, about an inch from the front; PUSH baby-bottle brushes through, with brush handles standing up, and PUSH flaps down. COVER top with paper. GLUE together cardboard circles with sticker letters over ends of brush handles.

3. CUT a cleaning cloth into fringe, and GLUE to back. USE an aluminum pan, cut to size, or foil for the floor.

SERVICE STATION HOW-TO

to make vacuum and air pumps

1. For a vacuum, GLUE colored paper to cover a toilet-paper tube, then decorate with stickers and painter's tape.

2. To make a hose, CUT the accordion sections out of flexible straws, and TAPE them together. PUNCH a hole in tube, and INSERT hose.

3. For an air pump, GLUE colored paper to cover a raisin box, then DECORATE with stickers; use stickers to turn a semicircle of paper into a gauge and GLUE in place. A cut rubber band affixed to the box is the hose.

to make gas pump

1. COVER a matchbox with foil.

2. POKE a hole in the side; INSERT a rubber band, and GLUE on nozzle-shaped piece of cardboard.

3. GLUE small strips of black paper to pieces of cardboard, then GLUE these to front and back of pumps.

MINIATURE SKI SCENE

The distinctive shape of a supermarket ham can—tall and domed, several inches deep—makes a great frame for a diorama. This one features a mountainside scene complete with tiny skiers hitting the slopes. Cookie and biscuit tins, which also come in fun shapes, work just as well for this project.

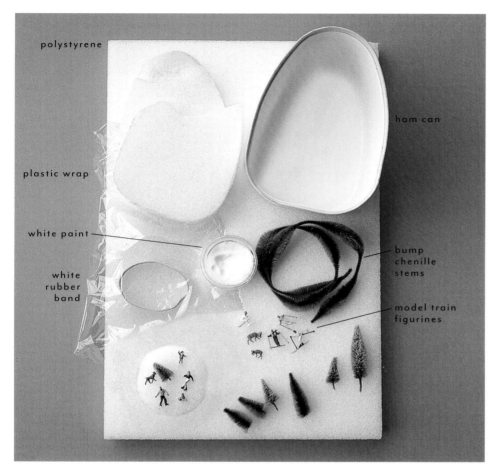

polystyrene

ham can

plastic wrap

white paint

bump chenille stems

white rubber band

model train figurines

SUPPLIES:

- Pencil
- Well-washed and dried ham can or cookie tin
- ½-inch-thick polystyrene
- Serrated knife
- All-purpose glue or hot-glue gun and glue stick
- Bump chenille stems in green
- Paintbrush
- White craft glue
- Borax (or white paint)
- Model train figurines of deer and skiers
- Plastic wrap
- White rubber band
- Toothbrush
- White paint

STEPS:

1. TRACE outline of ham can onto a piece of ½-inch-thick polystyrene (available at crafts stores) five times.

2. An adult should use a serrated knife to CUT the polystyrene: The background layer should be full size; CUT four increasingly lower slopes from the other layers. GLUE in place.

3. TRIM bump chenille stems to make trees, cutting bristles off bottom ¼ inch of each for a trunk. To dust trees with snow, BRUSH on white glue and SPRINKLE with borax, or spatter on white paint. POKE trees into sloped sides of foam.

4. GLUE figurines into position on slopes and STRETCH plastic wrap over the container, securing with a rubber band. Using a toothbrush, SPATTER the plastic wrap with white paint for snow.

COOKIE COTTAGES

Imagine Candy Land come to life: houses made with cookie walls, gumdrop bushes, and lollipop lampposts. You can create a whole village—with dripping icicles of icing and coconut snowdrifts—using edible materials. These no-bake houses all start with the same basic graham-cracker structure, "glued" together with royal icing.

sweet chalet
Green and white candy wafers stand in for shingles on this Swiss-style home. Hang a green ring candy for a wreath on the door, and attach a piece of sourbelt candy for a ribbon. Stack green gumdrops for shrubs, and anchor a red lollipop in a red gumdrop for a lamppost. Lay down a couple of strips of red-and-white-striped gum leading up to the door.

to make royal icing

INGREDIENTS:

- 4 cups (1-pound box) confectioners' sugar
- ¼ cup plus 1 tablespoon meringue powder
- ¼ cup plus 3 tablespoons water, plus more if needed

DIRECTIONS:

Beat sugar, meringue powder, and the water with a mixer on low speed until smooth, about 7 minutes, adding more water, 1 tablespoon at a time, as needed. Use immediately.

MAKES ABOUT 2½ CUPS

SUPPLIES:

- Serrated knife
- Graham cracker sheets
- Resealable plastic bag
- Scissors
- Royal icing recipe and ingredients (above right)
- Paper plate
- Small jar
- Assorted candies, for decorating details
- Shredded coconut

BASIC STEPS:

1. With a serrated knife, an adult should SAW 1 graham cracker sheet in half to create 2 squares; these will be the sides of the cottage. SAW off top corners of 2 more sheets, as pictured, to create a peaked roof; these will be the front and back pieces.

2. Using a resealable plastic bag with a corner snipped off, PIPE icing onto bottom and straight edges of a peaked piece. PLACE on an upside-down paper plate, using a small jar to prop it up. PIPE icing onto edges of a square piece, and ADHERE it to peaked piece. REMOVE jar, and ADHERE other pieces with icing, placing peaked pieces across from each other.

3. SAW another sheet into 2 squares for the roof. If desired, SPREAD icing onto roof pieces and DECORATE with candy to mimic shingles; let dry. PIPE icing onto top edges of house, and ADHERE roof pieces. ADD other decorative details as desired. SURROUND with coconut "snow."

to make a peppermint place

For the house, which is studded with cinnamon candies, you'll need to layer same-size strips of sourbelt candies to cover the roof. Add a heart-shaped candy-cane window and a graham-cracker door. You can build a "snowman" by stacking peppermint candies and make a mailbox with a swirl candy, a piece of a candy cane, and a gumdrop. Cut a flag for the mailbox from a stick of gum. To make your own little sleigh rider, slice off the top and bottom of a white gumdrop, and press it onto a soft swirl candy; use a piece of red gumdrop for a hat and two black nonpareils for eyes. Set a graham cracker atop 2 candy canes to make the sleigh.

COOKIE COTTAGES HOW-TO

to make a tiny tudor

Spread the outside walls of the house with a thick layer of royal icing for a "stucco" finish. While icing is wet, add pretzel-stick timbers and a dark brown roof and door made with chocolate graham crackers. Heap some hazelnut rolled-wafer cookie logs against one wall. For the doormat, use alphabet pasta to spell out "welcome" on another chocolate graham cracker. Add pasta numbers to embellish the door, and a pretzel for a knob. The fence—pretzel sticks glued together with icing—will stand up if you bury a piece of each post in drifts of coconut snow.

to make a woodland hideaway

Nestled in a sugar-cone forest, this cozy cabin has blanched almond slices for roof shingles and a roasted pumpkin seed in its shell for an attic window. Pile cinnamon-stick logs against an outside wall and erect a chimney made from a stack of caramels behind the house. Use a sesame bar to line the front path, and finish with a jellybean doorknob.

CARDBOARD WORLDS

With these easy-to-build, fold-away cardboard structures, you can create a host of charming little playscapes. We set up a living room, classroom, and barn, but there's no end to what you can make.

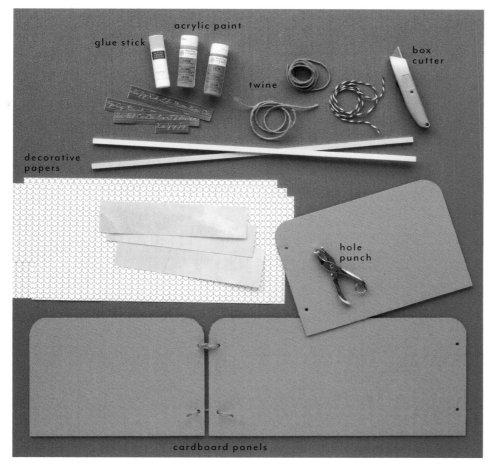

SUPPLIES:

- Scissors
- Cardboard Worlds templates (see page 331)
- Pencil
- Corrugated cardboard (box or sheet)
- Box cutter
- Wallpaper or other decorative papers
- White craft glue or glue stick
- Acrylic paint
- Hole punch
- Wood veneer (for floor; optional)
- Yarn or heavy twine
- Dollhouse furniture and accessories (store-bought or homemade)

STEPS:

1. CUT out templates and TRACE onto corrugated cardboard. An adult should use the box cutter to CUT out pieces.

2. CUT wallpaper to fit and attach to cardboard with glue, and/or PAINT the walls, as desired. Let dry.

3. USE a hole punch to punch two holes on each end of the long wall (1½ inches from top and bottom of cardboard), and two on one end of each short wall at corresponding heights. TIE pieces together with yarn or twine to make hinged walls. Ask an adult to CUT holes for a door and windows as desired, then HINGE the door with holes and yarn as for the walls.

4. SET up the house on a "floor" of wood-veneer or colored paper, if desired, then ADD furniture, dolls, and other accessories.

cardboard schoolhouse

This well-equipped classroom features a chalkboard (a mini frame with chalkboard-painted interior), a butterfly shadowbox, and science specimens in jars atop the bookcase. Kids can create miniature works of art (or shrink life-size ones with a photocopier or scanner) to glue to walls and accessories like the tiny cardboard laptop. Add miniature letter stencils and maps along a picture ledge (made by attaching balsa-wood strips to wood-veneer paper, both available at crafts stores). Don't forget an apple (ours is made from clay) for the teacher!

cardboard barn

Red-painted walls make this barn feel more lifelike. A big, swinging double door allows livestock to move in and out with ease. Populate your barn with wooden or plastic toy animals, ladders, and fences, and feed the animals some shredded paper "hay."

did you know?

Lots of tiny accessories and decorative touches, such as wood-veneer paper for walls and flat wood strips for shelves, can be found in the dollhouse section of crafts stores. It's fun to fill your cardboard house with a combination of dollhouse pieces, toys you scavenge from other games, and details you make yourself—craft a cardboard piano, a bowl of clay fruit, or some curtains out of fabric samples.

MAKE YOUR OWN FUN

You won't find these toys in any store. With some ingenuity and a few ordinary household objects, you can fashion musical instruments, toys, games, and much more.

MAKING MUSIC

Aspiring musicians, take note: To start your own band, just raid the kitchen junk drawer and the recycling bin. Each is likely filled with the makings of simple instruments. Craft a banjo from rubber bands strung on an old shoe box, a tambourine from paper plates and bottle caps, a drum from an empty coffee can, or a paper-tube kazoo.

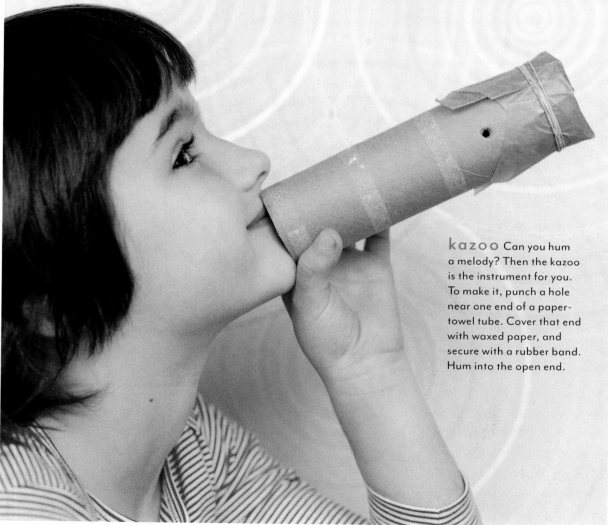

drum A ribbon knotted inside a large empty can allows you to march to your own tune while you drum. For each drumstick, ask an adult to use a hammer and nail to poke a hole in a ping-pong ball, then you can push a wooden dowel into the hole.

kazoo Can you hum a melody? Then the kazoo is the instrument for you. To make it, punch a hole near one end of a paper-towel tube. Cover that end with waxed paper, and secure with a rubber band. Hum into the open end.

TAMBOURINE HOW-TO

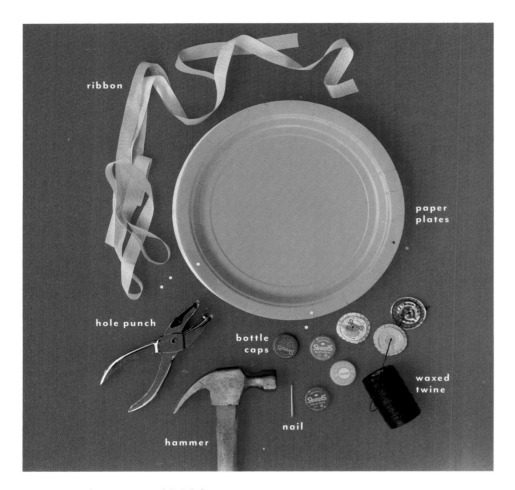

ribbon

paper plates

hole punch

bottle caps

waxed twine

hammer

nail

SUPPLIES:

- Hammer and nail
- Approximately 20 metal bottle caps
- White craft glue
- 2 stiff paper plates
- Hole punch
- Waxed twine or yarn
- Ribbon or seam-binding

STEPS:

1. An adult should help with this step: On a sturdy work surface, HAMMER the bottle caps flat. For the fullest sound, MAKE some of them flatter than others. HAMMER a nail hole in the middle of each cap.

2. GLUE paper plates together with their bottoms facing; let dry.

3. PUNCH 6 pairs of holes around the rims of the plates. Through 5 pairs of holes, THREAD 4 inches of waxed twine or yarn, positioning pairs and trios of bottle caps between and outside the plates to MAKE little stacks of jingles, and TIE.

4. TIE ribbon streamers through the last hole (as shown on page 104).

BANJO HOW-TO

Labels in image: mailing tube · large rubber bands · utility knife · pencil · shoe box

did you know?
For a banjo or any stringed instrument, a bridge is key. Wrap a cardboard shoe box with rubber bands, strum, and you get nothing—barely a twang. But lift those bands with a pair of pencils and suddenly you're playing a tune.

SUPPLIES:

- 2 pencils
- Shoe box with attached lid
- Glass jar or lid
- Utility knife
- Mailing tube
- Rubber bands in various sizes, including very large

STEPS:

1. DRAW a circle onto center of the lid of a shoe box, using a jar or lid as your tracing guide; ask an adult to CUT out the circle with a utility knife.

2. TRACE another circle around a mailing tube onto one short side of the shoe box; CUT just inside the tracing, and PUSH the tube through the hole for the banjo's neck.

3. STRETCH the rubber bands all the way around the shoe box. CREATE a bridge by placing 2 pencils on top of the shoe box, one on each side of the cutout, under the rubber bands (without a bridge, your banjo won't work; see tip above). Rubber bands of different lengths and widths will give you different notes.

CRAFTY CARS

Ready? Set? Go! Car lovers of all ages delight in making their own vehicles, and just about anything they can attach to a set of wheels has driving potential. An empty plastic bottle, say, or even an empty popcorn box can easily become a race car.

air power Talk about blowing away the competition! This carton is outfitted with four wheels and a balloon on top that you can inflate and then release for a quick whoosh of speed. Start with a clean cardboard popcorn container.

POPCORN RACER HOW-TO

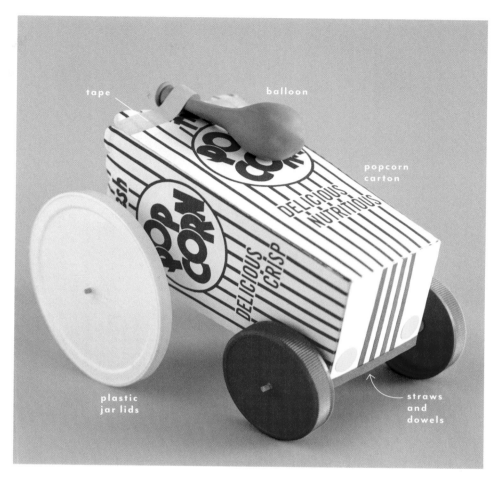

tape

balloon

popcorn
carton

plastic
jar lids

straws
and
dowels

SUPPLIES:

· Tape
· Balloon
· Popcorn carton
· 2 wooden skewers
· 2 drinking straws
· Awl
· 4 plastic jar
  or bottle lids
· Washer (for
  balance;
  optional)

STEPS:

1. Loosely TAPE a balloon to the top of a popcorn carton so that air can pass underneath it.

2. For the wheels, SLIDE 2 skewers through 2 straws (the skewers should be thinner and slightly longer than the straws). An adult should use an awl to PUNCTURE a small hole in each of 4 plastic jar or bottle lids (4 of the same size or 2 sets of different sizes).

3. SLIDE the ends of skewers into the holes of lids. TAPE the straws to the bottom of carton. If the car seems unbalanced, TAPE a washer to carton's bottom or side. REV up the "engine" by inflating the balloon, and then let go and watch it race away.

BOTTLE HOT ROD HOW-TO

SUPPLIES:

- Plastic bottle
- 4 wheels (from broken toys, or use plastic jar or bottle lids)
- 2 wooden skewers
- 3 drinking straws
- Awl
- Washer (for balance; optional)
- Tape
- Stickers
- Red tape
- Scissors

STEPS:

1. REMOVE label from plastic bottle.

2. USE the technique on page 111 to ATTACH wheels from broken toys to bottle using skewers, straws, and tape.

3. DECK out your ride with number and star stickers, and ADD a racing flag made of a straw and red tape cut into a triangle.

repurposed racer
Raid the recycling bin for bottles. Experiment with different shapes and sizes, and race them to see which goes fastest.

These crafts are for kids who love to make things move—miniature cars and buses, trains and planes, rocket ships and UFOs. In an afternoon, you can turn cereal boxes, paper plates, and cardboard tubes into vehicles of all sorts. And you don't need any high-tech materials—just flour, strips of newspaper, glue, and paint.

flying objects
Googly-eyed aliens ride
aboard out-of-this-world
flying saucers. Suspended
from clear monofilament,
they speed through space
passing a rocket ship
from earth on the way.

PAPIER-MÂCHÉ VEHICLES HOW-TO

to make the base

1. LOOK around the house for lightweight cardboard containers the right shape and size for your base and other parts. You can manipulate the shape of each box—we opened the corners of one to make windshields. TAPE boxes together to secure.

2. To make wheel shapes, POKE holes in box with a pencil, and SLIDE chopsticks through as a place holder; CUT out rounds from cardboard. For spinning wheels, CUT straws a bit wider than car and use to replace chopsticks; SLIP on cardboard wheels.

to cover with papier-mâché

1. MAKE the papier-mâché mixture by blending I part flour with 2 parts water in a bowl, and STIR until smooth.

2. TEAR or cut newspaper into strips. DIP a piece of newspaper into the mixture; SQUEEZE with your fingers so it isn't drippy. LAY paper over vehicle base; gently smooth. CONTINUE until the outside is a few layers thick. Let dry overnight.

3. Once dry, PAINT with tempera or acrylic. GLUE on any details, stickers, and other decorative items. ATTACH wheels; TRIM chopsticks.

tip ✳

Papier-mâché can get a little messy, so be sure to completely cover your work space with paper before beginning.

to make a rocket

1. For an irregular shape like the rocket's, SQUEEZE crumpled newspaper into a tapered shape, and TAPE in place on top of a short cardboard tube.

2. CUT out wing shapes from lightweight cardboard boxes and TAPE into place, then cover rocket and wings with papier-mâché as directed, opposite. Let dry overnight.

3. PAINT rocket with tempera or acrylic, then DECORATE with stickers, rickrack, and other decorative items.

to make a flying saucer

1. CUT a hole in the center of a paper plate, making it large enough to hold a small paper cup.

2. PLACE the paper plate with the hole and another paper plate together with their tops facing (STUFF crumpled newspaper inside to support the sagging surface). TAPE together and cover with papier-mâché as directed, opposite. Let dry overnight.

3. PAINT with tempera or acrylic, then DECORATE with stickers and tape. When dry, PLACE an alien inside the cup, and TAPE down a pastic container (clean fruit cups or drink covers are just the right size).

PEG-BOARD MARBLE RUN

Lots of kids like to tinker with machines, take things apart, and generally figure out how stuff works—just for fun. Embrace that curiosity with this endlessly fascinating project. It involves creating a clacking, whacking gumball machine that runs without electricity, all with parts found in the kitchen and toy box. This gadget starts up with the turn of a paddle, and then—after much rolling and pushing and lifting—drops a gumball into a container. You win!

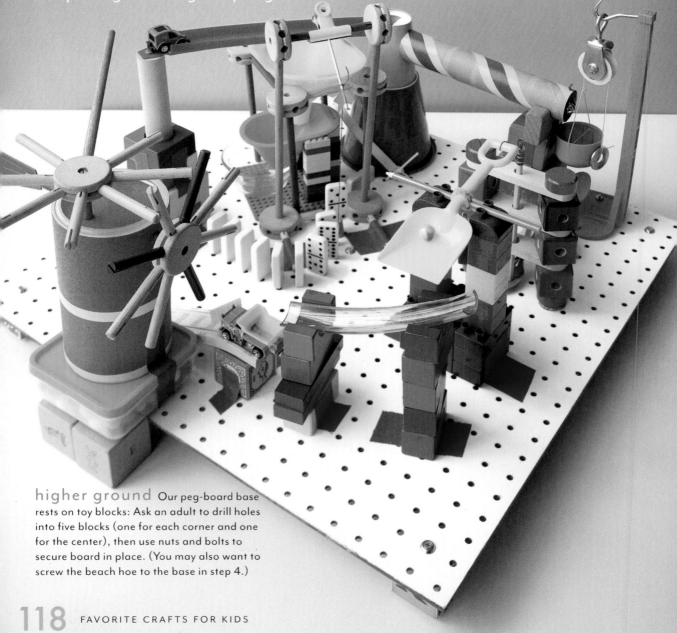

higher ground Our peg-board base rests on toy blocks: Ask an adult to drill holes into five blocks (one for each corner and one for the center), then use nuts and bolts to secure board in place. (You may also want to screw the beach hoe to the base in step 4.)

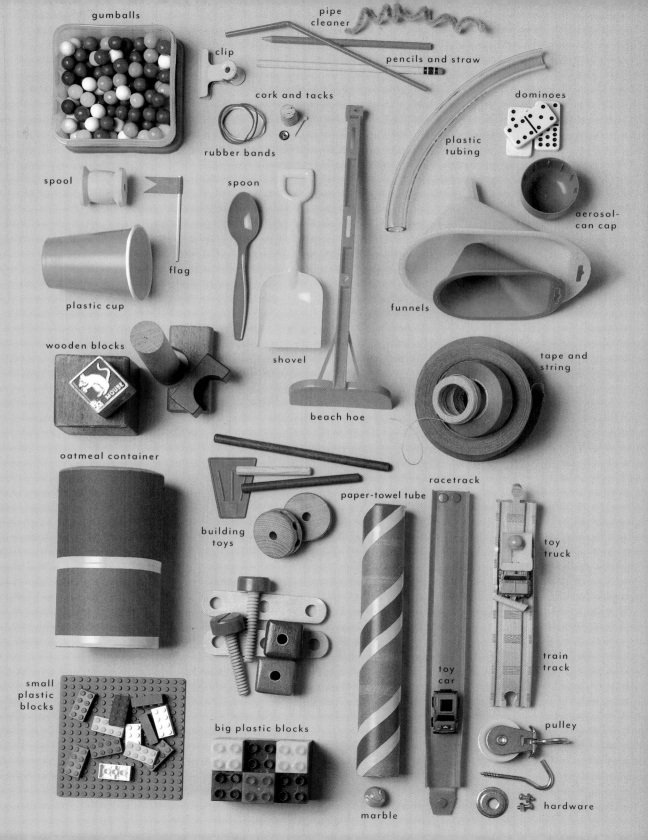

gumballs

pipe cleaner

clip

pencils and straw

cork and tacks

rubber bands

dominoes

plastic tubing

spool

spoon

aerosol-can cap

flag

plastic cup

funnels

wooden blocks

shovel

tape and string

beach hoe

oatmeal container

building toys

paper-towel tube

racetrack

toy truck

train track

small plastic blocks

big plastic blocks

toy car

pulley

hardware

marble

gear

ramp

pulley

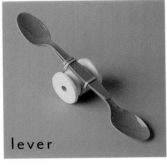

lever

① 1

tip ✳

To keep the marble in motion you need four basic machine parts:

- A **gear** is a wheel with spokes that fit together with another gear and push on it to make it turn.

- A **ramp** moves objects from a higher to a lower place, and things gain momentum as they go down.

- A **pulley** transports loads up or down (it's a wheel with a groove that has a string slung over it).

- A **lever** is like a seesaw: Put weight on one end, and the other rises.

did you know?

Complicated contraptions that operate by chain reactions to perform simple tasks are known as "Rube Goldberg machines," after an American cartoonist who perfected the art. They are fun to build and can be small enough to fit on a table or big enough to fill a room and then some.

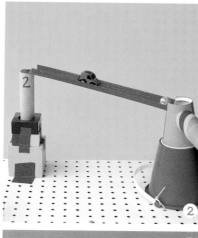

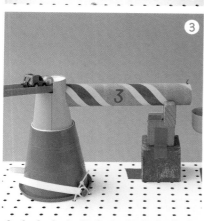

STEPS:

1. START with a gear (see opposite). The side wheel's shaft goes through the oatmeal container to a paddle made with building toys (see page 123). When you TURN the paddle, the gear's spokes rotate the top wheel, which has one long spoke.

2. This causes the car to ROLL down the ramp and into a marble (held in place by 2 tacks) on the ramp's lower end.

3. The marble KNOCKS through a hole in the top of an upside-down cup and into a paper-towel tube (which is pushed into a hole in the cup's side). The marble ROLLS through the tube.

4. On the marble's way out of the tube, it FALLS into an aerosol-can cap. The cap is at one end of a pulley's string (the other end has a washer tied to it). The pulley hangs from a hook attached to a beach hoe. The weight of the marble PLUNKS the cap onto one end of a lever (made of spoons fastened to a spool).

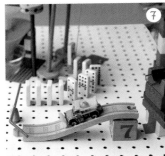
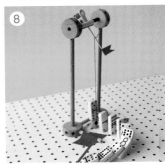

5. The weight of the marble on one end of the lever causes the other end to BUMP a pencil attached to a shovel handle with a tack and string. This LIFTS the handle, which TIPS a marble resting in the shovel.

6. The marble ROLLS down into another ramp made from plastic tubing. At the end, it DROPS into the back of a truck parked on a lower ramp.

7. The weight causes the truck to ROLL down a piece of train track and STRIKE a bendable straw, which SWINGS into a series of upright dominoes.

8. The dominoes TOPPLE one by one. The last domino weighs down a cork TACKED to a string, which is tied to a flag. The flag is ATTACHED to a clip; PERCHED on the clip is a gumball.

9. When the last domino FALLS, the cork is released, and the flag pops up. The gumball on the clip FALLS and drops through 2 funnels, then into a bowl. The machine finally comes to a stop.

tips

Your machine's parts are less likely to break down if you follow a few suggestions:

- Be sure the sections are high in the beginning and gradually get lower—then go up again in the middle—to provide momentum.

- Use strong tape to anchor objects to the surface (ours is a piece of Peg-Board).

- Keep joints from wiggling by tightening them with rubber bands, twist ties, or pipe cleaners. If something isn't working after an adjustment, don't be afraid to replace the structure with new elements (for instance, use blocks instead of construction toys).

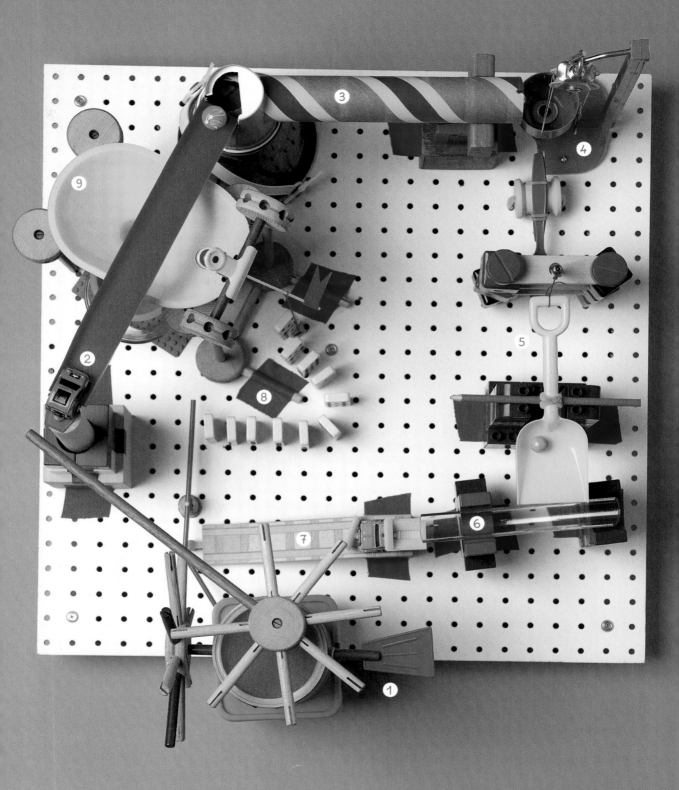

FORTUNE
TELLERS

Folded paper fortune tellers
are a schoolyard staple. Make
one to let your friends know
what is in store for them.
For extra-fancy versions, use
patterned origami
paper instead of plain.

HOW-TO

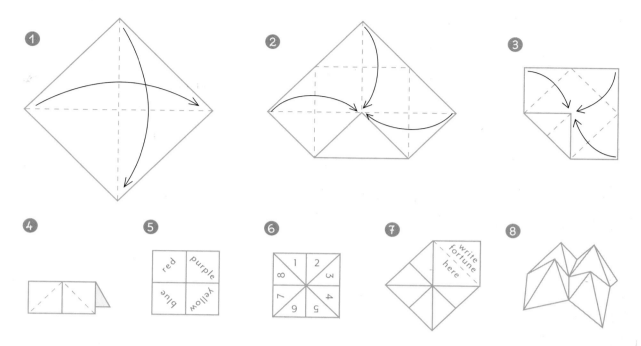

STEPS:

1. FOLD a square piece of paper in half, then in half again. OPEN, and SMOOTH flat.

2. FOLD each of the 4 corners into the center, creating a smaller square.

3. TURN the paper over and FOLD the corners into the center again, creating an even smaller square.

4. FOLD the paper in half and UNFOLD; FOLD in half the other way and UNFOLD. Write words, letters, or numbers on each of the 4 flaps and the 8 triangles inside the teller; write "fortunes" underneath those triangles.

5. INSERT your thumbs and index fingers into the 4 square flaps on one side, and MOVE your fingers back and forth, opening the fortune teller's "mouth" in alternating directions.

how to use a paper fortune teller

Set it up: We wrote colors on the 4 flaps and numbers on the 8 triangles inside the teller, but you can use months of the year, or any other words you like. Underneath those 8 triangles, write creative fortunes that will be fun for your friends to read.

Tell a fortune: Have someone choose one of the words from the first 4 flaps, then open/close the teller in time for each letter in that word; repeat twice, with the words, letters, or numbers on the inside triangles. Finally, have the person choose from the inside triangles once more. Lift that flap to reveal the fortune beneath.

PAPER AIRPLANES

Paper airplanes can take any shape you like—from supersonic jets to old-fashioned propeller planes. The fliers on these pages are designed to do all kinds of tricks. Tinker with how they are folded to get them soaring. Make a stand from wire to display each plane when it's grounded.

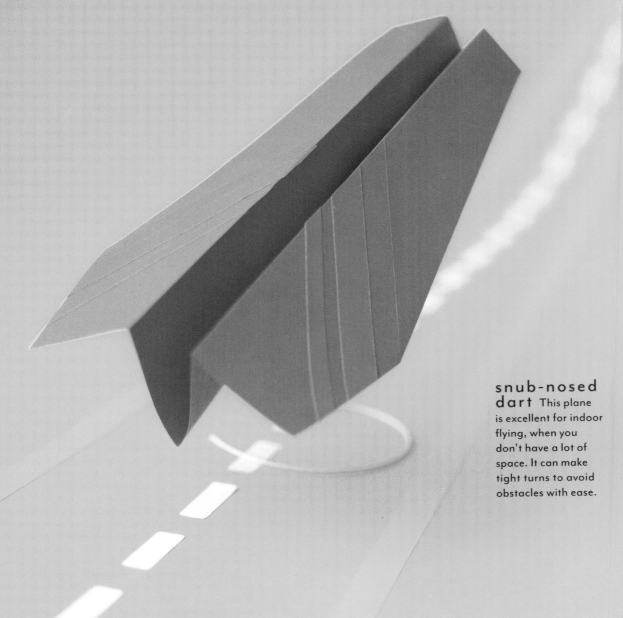

snub-nosed dart This plane is excellent for indoor flying, when you don't have a lot of space. It can make tight turns to avoid obstacles with ease.

SNUB-NOSED DART HOW-TO

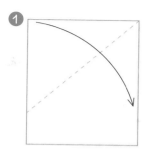
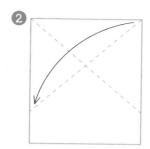
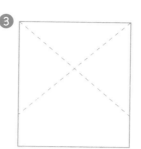
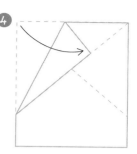

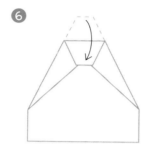
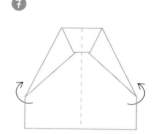

STEPS:

1. PLACE an 8½-by-11-inch piece of paper in front of you with a short side toward you. FOLD the upper left corner down to meet the right edge, and OPEN.

2. FOLD the upper right corner down to meet the left edge.

3. OPEN and SMOOTH flat.

4. FOLD the upper left side down so its edge meets the diagonal crease.

5. FOLD the upper right side down so its edge meets the other diagonal crease.

6. FOLD the tip down so that its corners meet the inner edges of the two angled folds.

7. FOLD the paper in half lengthwise so that the folded tip is on the outside.

8. The edge with the folded tip is the bottom of the plane. FOLD the two upper edges down to meet the bottom edge to form the wings. OPEN wings slightly.

tip

Stickers give a paper plane a little extra panache—a striped wing, for example, or a star on the tail. Of course, you can simply leave it unadorned and let the sleek craft speak for itself.

This plane should need only a little adjustment to the wing tips; fold back edges up slightly if it dives or fold them down slightly if it stalls.

DELTA WING HOW-TO

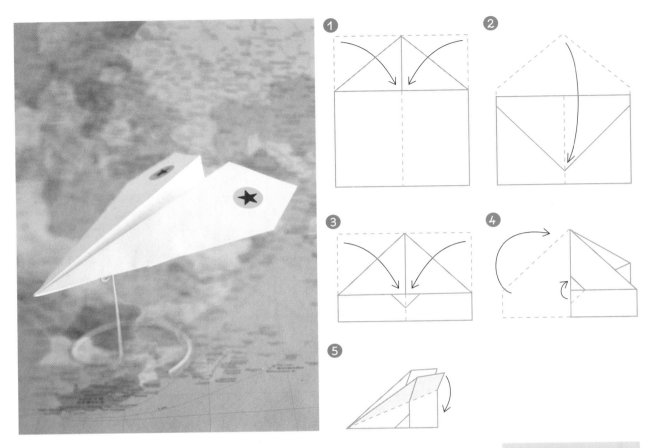

STEPS:

1. Place an 8½-by-11-inch piece of paper flat with a short side toward you; FOLD in half lengthwise. OPEN, and smooth flat. FOLD upper corners down to meet center crease.

2. FOLD top of paper down so that its tip falls about an inch from the bottom edge.

3. FOLD the two upper corners down to meet center crease.

4. FOLD up the triangular tip that sticks out. FOLD the plane in half so that the triangular tip is on the outside.

5. The edge with the little triangle is the bottom of the plane. FOLD the angled upper edges down to meet the bottom to form the wings. OPEN so the wings go up like the steep arms of a Y.

tip

If the plane dives, bend the backs of the wings up slightly to slow it down. Bend the plane's tail, or rudder, to turn left or right.

AIRPLANE STAND HOW-TO

STEPS:

1. To form the base, an adult should CUT a 16-inch piece of 18-gauge wire. CURL the wire around the bottom of a drinking glass to create a loose circle about 3 inches across. Holding the circle flat on your work surface, BEND the remaining wire straight up.

2. CURL the end of the wire twice around a pencil or pen to create 2 loops.

3. CLIP the body of a plane between the loops to hold it.

tip

You may have to bend the upper loops a little to the left or right to center the plane over the base (otherwise it will tip over). Also, the clip should grasp the plane toward the back to create the best balance.

PAPER POM-POMS

Pump up the crowd with these handheld puffs, made from layered tissue paper cut in strips and wrapped around dowels. Use your favorite team colors or any festive combination. Add extra layers for super-large pom-poms, or tape skinny strips to both ends of a longer dowel for a spirited baton. Hip, hip, hurrah!

SUPPLIES:

- Tissue paper in various colors
- Scissors
- Short ¼-inch-diameter dowels
- Vinyl tape

STEPS:

1. STACK 4 sheets of tissue paper on top of each other, then FOLD them in half and cut 1-inch-wide strips through all layers, stopping just short of the fold so that strips will hold together.

2. Starting at one corner, ROLL the folded edge tightly around one end of a dowel and SECURE bottom of pom-pom to dowel with vinyl tape.

3. REPEAT entire process, beginning with 4 more sheets of tissue paper, at least two more times to make the ball fluffy.

BEACH BOARD GAMES

For a portable version of classic board games, try making
a roll-up board from a place mat. Stamp one side with
a checkerboard and the other with a tic-tac-toe grid. When
the fun is over, shake off the fabric and toss it in your beach bag.

game pieces Before you
play, go on a hunt for game pieces:
Stones, shells, even larger pieces of
sea glass will work—assign lighter-
hued pieces to one player, and darker
ones to the other.

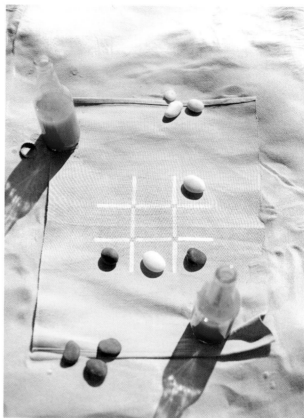

SUPPLIES:

- Ruler
- Disappearing-ink fabric pen
- Fabric place mat
- Vinyl eraser
- Fabric paint
- Utility knife (optional)

STEPS:

1. Using a ruler and a disappearing-ink pen, DRAW guidelines for tic-tac-toe on the back and checkers on the front of a fabric place mat.

2. Then DIP a vinyl eraser into fabric paint and STAMP the design along the guidelines. Work in rows for the checkerboard, stamping every other square. (An adult may have to use a utility knife to CUT the eraser to an appropriate shape; for thinner lines, such as those on the tic-tac-toe grid, USE the side of the eraser.) Let dry.

BALL-IN-THE-HOLE GAMES

Modern-day gizmos don't hold a candle to these sweet, old-fashioned dime-store toys when it comes to capturing a kid's attention. Remember: The more beads you add, the more difficult the challenge.

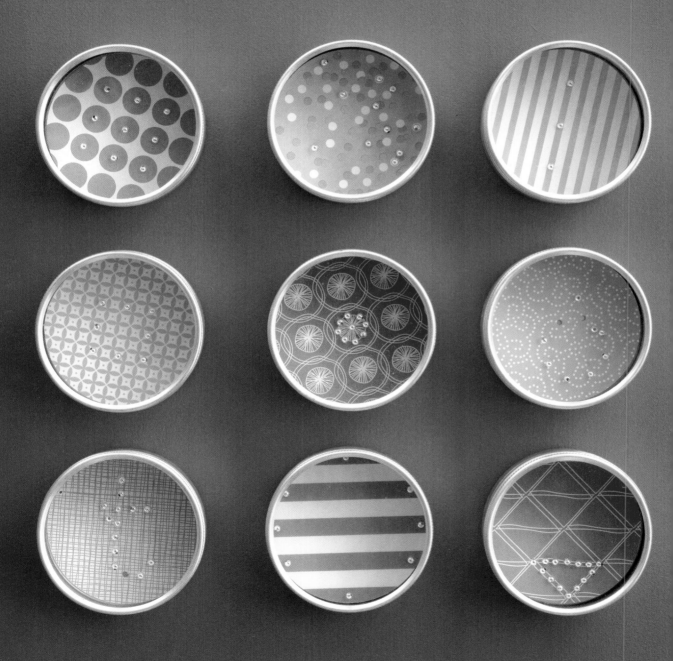

patterned
paper

glue stick

cardboard

screw punch

silver seed
beads

watchmaker box

SUPPLIES:

- Pencil
- Watchmaker boxes
  (available at crafts stores
  and online)
- Lightweight cardboard
- Patterned paper
- Scissors or utility knife
- Glue stick
- Screw punch
- Silver seed beads (same
  size as hole punch)

STEPS:

1. TRACE around the circumference of a watchmaker box on cardboard and patterned paper, and CUT out circles.

2. GLUE paper to cardboard, then USE a screw punch to create a pattern of holes in the surface. (Note: You can use an ordinary hole punch, but you will be limited by the depth of the tool and may not be able to reach the center of your circle.)

3. GLUE circle paper-side-up inside box, then ADD as many silver seed beads as you have holes in your pattern. TOP box with lid.

BINGO!

This church-hall standby is a great diversion for groups of all ages—and a nice way for little ones to brush up on their knowledge of letters and numbers.

SUPPLIES:

- Letter and number stickers or marker
- Ping-Pong balls
- Bingo! templates (see page 331)
- Card stock in white plus various colors (for making chips)
- ¾-inch circle punch

STEPS:

1. To mark the bingo balls, ATTACH letter and number stickers to Ping-Pong balls (or simply WRITE them on with a marker). We gave our game kid-friendly small numbers: for "B," we used 1 through 6; "I," 7 through 12; "N," 13 through 18; "G," 19 through 24; and "O," 25 through 30.

2. To make the cards, DOWNLOAD the templates and PRINT onto white card stock.

3. Use a circle punch to CUT out the chips from colored card stock; you'll need about 20 for each player.

ROCK DOMINOES

Those smooth flat stones that are perfect for skipping are just right for game pieces, too. Collect 28 flat oval stones of approximately the same size and color and you can make your own set of dominoes. Paint a line across the center of each rock with a white paint pen. Then, on either side of the line, mark with a set of dots until you have a domino in every combination, from 0-0 to 6-6.

tip

Here's how to play the game: Start by shuffling the dominoes and laying them facedown, then each player draws seven dominoes. The player with the highest total number on a domino goes first and lays that one down. The next player places a domino with the same number next to the first domino at either end. Players take turns laying dominoes in this manner, with the same numbers always touching. If you don't have a domino that matches any of those in play, pick from the pile or pass if there are no more left to pick. The first player to run out of dominoes wins.

MAP PUZZLE

Here's a fun brain-teaser for any kid who loves studying geography, or for a train buff who enjoys checking out railway lines: a puzzle made from a map that you can put together and take apart—again and again.

SUPPLIES:

· Map
· Pencil
· Scissors
· Laminating paper

STEPS:

1. START with a color map, or DOWNLOAD and PRINT one (we used a map of the United States). With a pencil, DRAW lines freehand to make puzzle pieces.

2. CUT out pieces. COVER front and back with laminating sheets.

3. TRIM shapes with scissors, leaving ⅛-inch border of plastic all around each.

CARPET-TILE HOPSCOTCH

If it's raining, you can bring sidewalk games indoors. Carpet squares stack when not in use, and are much easier on the feet than concrete! Stencil large numbers onto 6 carpet tiles with fabric or latex paint, and let dry. Use a beanbag to play hopscotch.

ELEPHANT STILTS

It's a jungle in there—in the playroom, that is! Give tiny elephants a lift with a pair of tin-can feet. With a church-key can opener, make holes in the sides of 2 unopened 15-ounce cans. Then rinse cans thoroughly, remove labels, and let dry. Use black and pink acrylic paints to apply toenails. Cut a nylon stretch cord to about 60 inches for each foot, depending on child's height; thread it through holes, and knot.

GINGHAM DOLLS

These simple stuffed D.I.Y. dolls have old-
fashioned charm and are easy even for little
hands to assemble. (An adult may need
to help younger crafters with the cutting
and stitching; see page 144 for basic sewing
instructions.) Make a whole family of tiny
gingham dolls, and finish them with
details such as different length and color
of hair and accessories like a gingham-
ribbon tie.

HOW-TO

SUPPLIES:

- Gingham Dolls templates (see page 332)
- Scissors
- Gingham cotton fabric
- Steam iron
- Straight pins
- Fabric pencil
- Sewing machine and basic hand-sewing supplies
- Chopstick
- Polyester stuffing
- Needle and thread
- Embroidery floss
- Yarn scraps

STEPS:

1. Choose desired doll template and CUT out, or draw your own pattern and cut out. FOLD fabric in half with right sides facing; press with iron, and TRACE template onto fabric. CUT out for both layers, and pin.

2. Allowing a ¼-inch seam allowance, SEW almost all the way around the body. (LEAVE a 1-inch opening on the torso.)

3. TURN doll right side out, using a chopstick for corners. FILL with stuffing. (Use chopstick as needed to PUSH stuffing into arms and legs.) HAND-STITCH the side opening.

4. To embroider facial features: Use embroidery floss to MAKE a few backstitches to create eyes and a mouth.

5. To make the hair: For ponytails and braids, CUT 20 to 30 strands of yarn, about 12 inches long. DRAPE sideways over the head of the doll, and SEW at center (or slightly off center) to create a part. To leave hair long, STITCH onto doll across the back of the head. For ponytails, CLASP sides, and SECURE with a piece of yarn; STITCH onto the head at that point. For pigtails, BRAID the ponytails, and SECURE ends with another piece of yarn. For short hair, EMBROIDER all over the head using small backstitches.

BASIC SEWING TECHNIQUES

Every sewing project begins the same way: by threading a needle and tying a double knot. Beginners will find it easiest to practice with a single strand of embroidery floss and a needle with a large eye.

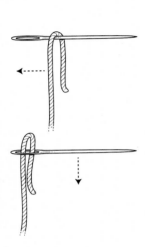

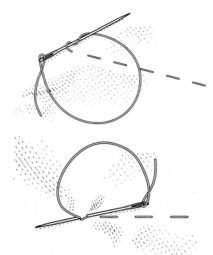

thread a needle

Take a 24-inch length of thread. Drape the thread over the needle, and hold both sides together to make a loop. Pull the needle up hard so it makes the loop pointy. Slide loop off needle. Slip the eye of the needle over the loop, and pull one end of the thread through. Tie a double knot at other end of the thread.

make an ending knot

When you reach the end or start to run out of thread, push the needle to the back of the fabric. Make three small stitches in the same spot. Before pulling the last one tight, slide the needle under the loop; pull the thread tight. Snip the thread.

sew a button

Hold the button in place on the fabric. Poke your needle up from the back of the fabric, through one hole, then down through the hole diagonally across from it. Repeat three or four times. Do the same with the remaining two holes (you'll create an X), ending with your thread at the back of the fabric. Pass the needle up through the fabric (but not through the button) and wrap around the thread beneath the button three times. Then pass the needle to the back of the fabric, and make an ending knot.

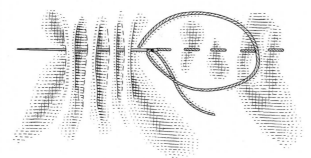

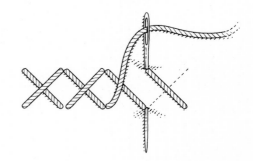

running stitch

Just as its name suggests, the running stitch zips along quickly. Pass the needle up from the back of your fabric, then go in and out of the fabric a few times. Gently pull the needle and thread through the fabric. Then repeat for the next stitches. At the end of your work, push the needle through to the back; make an ending knot.

cross-stitch

First, stitch a row of evenly spaced parallel diagonal lines. Then stitch diagonally back over the first row, creating crosses as you go. When you can, insert the needle where Xs meet in the same holes. For the entire pattern, the bottom stitches on each X should all slant one way and the top stitches the other way.

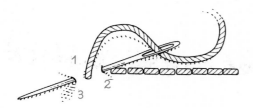

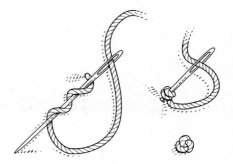

backstitch

The reason this is called the backstitch is that every new stitch starts in back of the thread. Pass the needle up from the back of your fabric, coming out at 1. Push the needle in at 2 and out at 3 of the fabric once, the same way you did for the running stitch (above). Pull the thread tight (you've just made your first stitch). Pass the needle down back near the end of the first stitch, and then up again a short distance in front of your thread. Repeat. Push the needle through to the back, and make an ending knot.

make a french knot

Insert the needle from the back to the front of the fabric. Keeping the thread taut with one hand, use your other hand to wind it over the needle twice. Reinsert the tip of the needle into the fabric, as close as possible to where it first emerged. Before passing the needle through the fabric, pull the thread tight so that the knot is flush with the material. Pull the needle through the fabric, continuing to hold the thread tight until you have a 3- to 4-inch loop, then let go, and finish the knot. For larger knots, wrap more than two times.

CORN-HUSK DOLLS

Corn-husk dolls evoke an earlier time, of life on the prairie or deep in the big woods. They are simple to construct with only a few essential supplies: dried corn husks (sold at many international grocers, for making tamales), and felt, raffia, and yarn for details.

HOW-TO

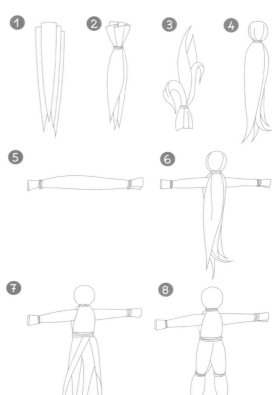

SUPPLIES:

- Dried corn husks
- Paper towels
- Thin twine
- Scissors
- Yarn or raffia
- Felt
- Fabric glue

STEPS:

1. SOAK husks in water 10 minutes; BLOT dry. STACK 4 or 6 husks (always an even number).

2. Using thin twine, TIE husks together, about 1 inch from top.

3. SEPARATE husks into equal portions (2 and 2, or 3 and 3), and FOLD halves down, covering twine.

4. Turn so twine is at top. Using thin twine, TIE husks about 1 inch down, creating head.

5. ROLL a single husk and tie at ends to make arms.

6. POSITION arms on doll: Place piece just below knot at neck, between equal portions of husks.

7. TIE waist just below arms. For female doll, TRIM husks to an even length.

8. For male doll, SEPARATE legs into equal portions. TIE at knees and ankles. TRIM evenly.

tip

Fashion clothes from felt: Cut rectangles, and snip slits or Xs in center; slide over head, and secure around waist with a strip of felt or yarn. Glue on small felt buttons; use scissors to make fringe. To make hair, glue yarn or raffia to the heads. Cut hats from felt, then glue in place.

STACK AND PLAY

A few inexpensive, assemble-it-yourself nightstands offer hours of endless fun when you transform them into a marketplace: Outfit one with a sun shade and caddies to hold supplies, and fill a stacked pair with extra goodies to sell. Later, when the shopping is done, that stacked unit can double as a puppet theater (see page 150).

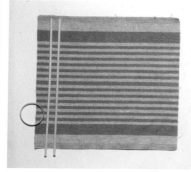

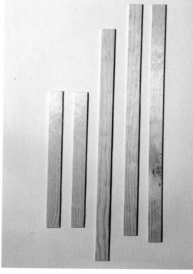

SUPPLIES:

· 3 small wooden nightstands (ours are from IKEA and measure 20½ by 11¾ by 15¾ inches)
· Cup hooks
· Cutlery caddy
· 1⅜-inch lattice strips
· Screws
· Small nails
· Hammer
· Tacky tape
· 2 dowels (21 inches long by ⁵⁄₁₆ inch wide)
· 1 yard fabric (for awning)
· Mending plates
· L-brackets

STEPS:

1. ASSEMBLE nightstands according to manufacturer's instructions, if necessary. SCREW 2 cup hooks into sides of unit to hold caddy (don't hang yet).

2. For awning, MAKE two crosses for sides using 1⅜-inch lattice strips: SCREW a 12-inch piece across a 47-inch piece 5 inches down from top. SECURE to side of table with one screw near the floor, another an inch below tabletop. REPEAT to make second cross. With small nails and a hammer, SPAN crosses with a 21-inch piece of lattice.

3. ATTACH tacky tape along dowels. STICK ends of a 21-inch-by-18-inch piece of fabric to the dowels; DRAPE over frame. HANG caddy.

4. For rear shelves, STACK and ATTACH 2 nightstands by screwing mending plates over the seams, front and back. (If desired, secure both assembled units to floor with L-brackets to keep from tipping.)

curtain call

Once the market has closed, why not catch a show? Those stacked shelves in the back of the store easily become a puppet theater with a few quick tweaks: A removable tension rod holds a curtain, a Velcro strip on the reverse supports a backdrop, and a chalkboard, hung from a cup hook on the middle shelf, hides the staging area.

Next
Show
4:30

PUPPET THEATER HOW-TO

SUPPLIES:

- Pair of stacked, attached nightstands (see Market How-To, page 149)
- 2 tea towels
- Fusible hem tape
- Iron
- Tension rod
- Adhesive Velcro
- Felt (we used 1 yard each of blue and green)
- Frame (ours is 20½ inches square)
- Chalkboard paint and paintbrush
- Cup hook
- L-brackets

STEPS:

1. MAKE curtains from 2 tea towels: MAKE a channel for the rod, FOLD over edge, and SECURE with fusible hem tape. SLIDE tension rod through curtains, and ADJUST for width of nightstand.

2. STICK adhesive-backed Velcro along the top edge of the back of unit. CUT a piece of blue felt to size of opening. DRAW a hillside on a piece of green felt (opposite) and CUT out. ATTACH to blue felt with fusible tape. STICK corresponding strip of Velcro along top.

3. REMOVE glass from frame. PAINT backing with chalkboard paint. SCREW a cup hook to underside of middle shelf, to hang frame.

TIN CAN TOYS

Connected together with bolts, washers, and nuts, empty cans come alive. Gather some clean ones in various shapes and sizes and then have an adult drill holes in them to get your project started. Your recycling bin just might hold the makings of a new best friend—a robot dog, cat, or mouse.

lap dog He's so well behaved, you can take this canine friend for a walk without a leash. Make the can's open end the tail end so you can hide the wing nuts that hold on its ears and body.

tips

- A heavy-duty can opener will create smoother edges than an ordinary one.

- Using our diagrams as a guide, first mark cans with a black permanent marker where drilled holes will go.

- An adult should drill holes with a $\frac{13}{64}$-inch bit.

- Extra-strong magnets work best for attaching metal decorations.

Spot

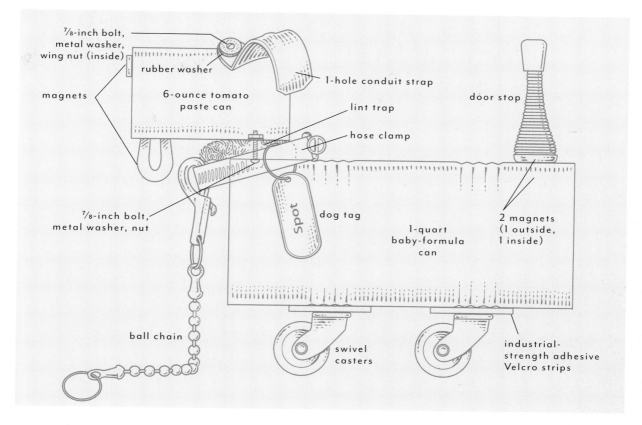

⅞-inch bolt, metal washer, wing nut (inside)

rubber washer

magnets

6-ounce tomato paste can

1-hole conduit strap

door stop

lint trap

hose clamp

⅞-inch bolt, metal washer, nut

spot

dog tag

1-quart baby-formula can

2 magnets (1 outside, 1 inside)

ball chain

swivel casters

industrial-strength adhesive Velcro strips

to make a dog:

1. For the legs: GLUE wheels to casters; ATTACH casters to large can with Velcro strips.

2. For the ears: DRILL 2 holes, about 1½ inches apart, one-third of the way from the open end of the small can. SMOOTH edges with sanding paper. AFFIX a conduit strap at each hole using a bolt, a washer, and a wing nut, which is fastened inside the can. The bolts that secure the ears will be the eyes; USE a rubber washer over the aluminum one to give the dog a "spot" around one of the eyes.

3. Attach head to body: DRILL a hole about ¾ inch from the closed end of the large can, and a corresponding hole in the side of the small can opposite the eyes, about 1 inch from the open end. SLIP a dog tag onto a hose clamp and PLACE clamp around a lint trap or scouring pad to create a neck with a collar. ATTACH the head to the body with a bolt and nut: INSERT the bolt from inside the large can, through the lint trap, and into the small can; SECURE with the nut. CLIP a ball chain to the clamp for a leash.

4. For the tail, ATTACH a small metal door stop to the open end of the large can with 2 magnets, one inside and one outside. USE a flat magnet for the nose and a horseshoe magnet for the tongue.

house cat

There's nothing finicky about this cute kitty; she'll take whatever scraps you "feed" her. Attach all parts to the cat's head before connecting it to the body. Ask an adult to do the drilling.

TIN CAN TOYS HOW-TO

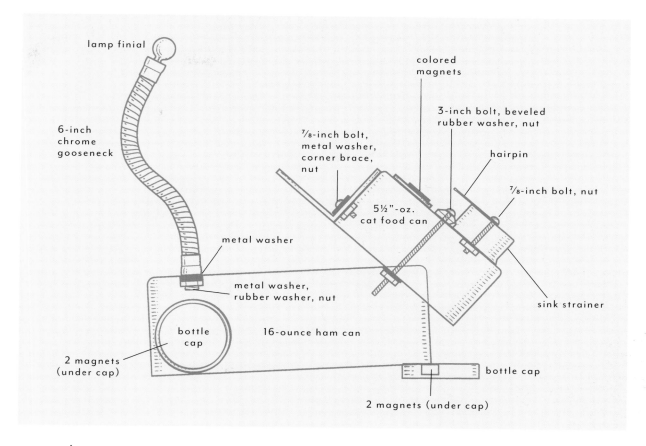

to make a cat:

1. Assemble head: For ears, DRILL 2 holes, about 2 inches apart, on side of can. AFFIX a corner brace to each hole with a bolt, washer, and nut, which is fastened inside can. For mouth, DRILL two holes, about 1½ inches apart, on bottom of can. AFFIX a sink strainer to each hole with a bolt and nut. SLIP a hairclip around each bolt for the whiskers.

2. DRILL hole in small can between strainers, and corresponding hole near narrow end of large can. ATTACH head to body with a long bolt, beveled rubber washer, and nut:

INSERT bolt from inside small can at an angle into large can; SECURE with nut.

3. For tail, DRILL a hole near wide end of large can, in center. ATTACH a lamp finial to one end of a gooseneck; THREAD other end through a metal washer and drilled hole plus a rubber washer and metal washer on inside of can; SECURE with nut.

4. For paws, ATTACH each of 4 bottle caps to the large can with 2 magnets: PLACE 2 caps underneath the narrow end and the other 2 on the sides at the wider end. ATTACH colored magnets on small can for the eyes.

pantry mouse

Squeak, squeak! Looks like this mouse has found his tin-can cheese. Even little ones can build this cute critter, since no drilling is required.

TIN CAN TOYS HOW-TO

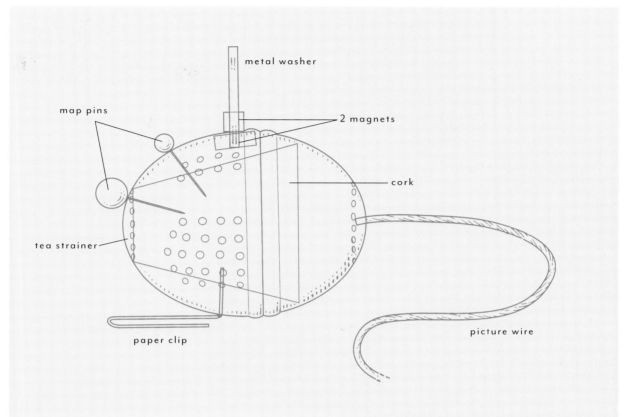

metal washer

map pins

2 magnets

cork

tea strainer

paper clip

picture wire

to make a mouse:

1. For the tail, TIE one end of a length of picture wire in a knot, then PUSH the other end through the bottom half of the tea strainer from the inside out.

2. PLACE a cork in the other half of the tea strainer as shown in the above diagram, and CLOSE strainer. PUSH 2 small map pins into holes of strainer and the cork for eyes; ADD a larger pin for the nose.

3. USE 2 magnets to attach metal washers for ears, placing 1 inside strainer and the other outside, between washers. For each paw, BEND one end of a paper clip and INSERT through hole into cork.

CHAPTER 4

DESIGN IT YOURSELF

Attention, fashion-forward kids: It's easy to make your own one-of-a-kind accessories, customized clothing, or awe-inspiring costumes. They'll brighten even rainy days.

PAINTED UMBRELLAS

Good-bye, rainy-day blues! Hello, cheerful umbrellas! These paint-it-yourself designs should put everyone in a sunny mood in no time. All you need is paint, brushes, a solid-colored nylon umbrella, and a burst of creativity.

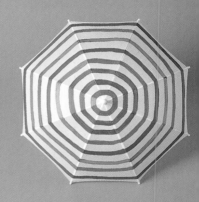

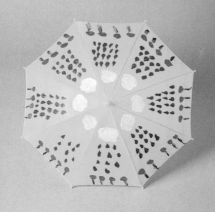

tip ✳

Read the manufacturer's directions on the paint before you begin: Some fabric paints require the addition of fixative; others require ironing the umbrella after painting it to "set" the design. Use a low heat setting and test the umbrella before ironing the painted portions; or iron with a press cloth over the pattern to protect the nylon.

SUPPLIES:

· Newspaper
· Smock
· Paintbrushes
· Fabric paint, or other permanent waterproof paint such as acrylic, in assorted colors
· Child-size nylon umbrella
· Disappearing-ink fabric pen

STEPS:

1. COVER the work surface with newspaper, and WEAR a smock to protect your clothes.

2. PAINT freehand designs onto umbrella or MARK a pattern with a disappearing-ink pen before you begin. TRY a simple repeating pattern, like stripes, polka dots, hearts, stars, numbers, or letters of the alphabet. The (cloudy) sky is the limit! Once finished, LEAVE the umbrella open overnight and allow the paint to dry completely before you close it or use it.

STENCILED
BACKPACK

The coolest backpack is definitely the one customized with your own initials. Plenty of bag-makers will create a monogram, but if you do the job yourself—giving the letters your own personal style—your bag will really stand out from the pack.

backpack

fabric paint

stencil brush

stencils

SUPPLIES:

· Backpack
· Cardboard letter stencils (available at hardware stores)
· Painter's tape
· Fabric paint
· Paper plate
· Stencil brush

STEPS:

1. UNZIP backpack and LAY flat on work surface. PLACE stencil in desired spot on backpack and TAPE to secure.

2. POUR a small amount of paint onto a paper plate. DIP end of stencil brush with paint, wipe off excess paint, and TAP brush over stencil to cover open areas completely.

3. LET paint dry completely and set according to manufacturer's instructions, then PEEL off stencil.

DUCT TAPE ACCESSORIES

Boys and girls alike need something sturdy to hold their allowance and other pocket money as well as holders for pencils, keys, and portable devices. This primary-colored gear is tough enough to stand up to just about any amount of wear and tear. Duct tape is strong and versatile, and when taped to itself (sticky sides in), it becomes a durable "fabric" that can be bent and taped into all sorts of useful shapes. Try experimenting with different colors and folded designs.

colorful catch-alls

Craft several accessories to fit all your needs. The examples here include coin purses, wallets, a pencil case, and several key chain pouches—just big enough to hold lunch money, an extra key, or a secret note.

HOW-TO

SUPPLIES:

- Duct tape in a variety of colors
- Scissors
- Pinking shears
- Self-adhesive Velcro
- Hole punch
- Key ring

STEPS:

1. CREATE duct tape "fabric" by sticking strips of tape together, with their sticky sides touching, so that one strip covers just half of the other widthwise. Then STICK another strip of tape to exposed half, again leaving half exposed. Continue to ADD tape in this overlapping fashion until you have a sheet the size you want. FOLD over the remaining flaps to finish the sheet.

2. TRIM the edges of the fabric with a pair of scissors to make them even. For decorative edges, TRIM them with pinking shears.

   For stripes, CUT strips of a different-colored duct tape to desired width, adhere to fabric, and trim edges. Use a hole punch to add decorative cutouts and embellishments.

3. FOLD the fabric into the shape you want (this one will be a wallet), and duct-tape the edges closed. ATTACH Velcro where needed to create a clasp. For a key chain, punch a hole for the ring.

TRAVEL TISSUES

Keep tissues at the ready with your very own personalized felt case, complete with a hand-stitched monogram on a tiny cut-out heart. Once you make yours, you may be inspired to make dozens more as gifts.

pretty pouches
Cut a 6¼-by-4¾-inch rectangle of felt with pinking shears; fold in short edges to meet at center. Sew ends with a running stitch. Backstitch an initial on a cut-out heart; apply with fabric glue.

NOTEBOOK AND PENCIL CASES

School supplies look even smarter when they're arranged in handcrafted cases. Each of these simple projects is made with two rectangles of felt—no hemming required. Refer to page 144 for basic sewing instructions.

Refer to page 144 for basic sewing instructions.

SUPPLIES:

- Scissors and pinking shears
- Felt
- Needle
- Embroidery floss
- Button
- 3-by-5-inch notebook

to make a pencil case

1. CUT a 2½-by-18-inch rectangle out of felt; FOLD bottom up 6 inches.

2. With a running stitch, SEW up sides.

3. FOLD over flap; ADD a button, as shown, and SNIP a buttonhole in the flap.

to cover a notebook

1. Using pinking shears, CUT an 11-by-5½-inch rectangle out of felt. CENTER open book on felt; FOLD ends over covers.

2. SEW top and bottom edges with running stitch.

3. SEW on a button and add a thread loop for a closure.

QUICK-STITCH PURSE

This stylish bag comes together so quickly you can make several for yourself and your friends in just one afternoon. Store-bought felt is super-easy to work with because it requires no hemming—trim a pretty edge with pinking shears and it will hold its shape.

SUPPLIES:

- Felt, in various colors
- Pinking shears
- Scissors (for details)
- Needle and thread
- Fabric glue
- Thick yarn or braided trim (for handles)
- Buttons (optional)

STEPS:

1. For each purse, use pinking shears to CUT 1 long rectangle of felt for a folded-over version (shown above right and lower left). Or CUT out 2 layers of felt in the same size (for the version shown opposite and above, top left).

2. STITCH or GLUE on decorations, such as the cherries and stems or daisy and leaf, before sewing the sides; do the same with handles made from store-bought trim.

3. USE a running stitch to join both sides (and bottom, if using 2 layers of felt), leaving the top open. To make a version with a flap, leave a portion of the top unstitched; fold flap over, and SEW on a button for a pretty detail.

FELTED-WOOL PURSES

Homemade felt can be used to create all sorts of accessories, like these colorful purses. This is wet work, so it's best to do it over (or near) a sink—or use a baking sheet with sides to catch any overflow.

did you know?

You can make fabric just by adding warm soapy water to wool roving (unspun wool)—no loom required. The same technique was used to make the finger puppets on page 36. It's called felting, a process of rubbing and tamping down warm, wet wool until it mats together into a sturdy material. If you've ever seen a wool sweater that was accidentally put in the washer and dryer, you've seen what happens: The fibers transform into something thick and dense, and in the case of felted wool, a material that's very workable.

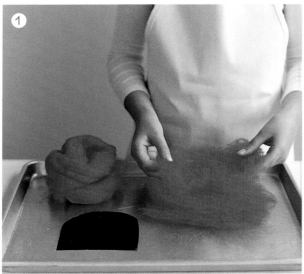

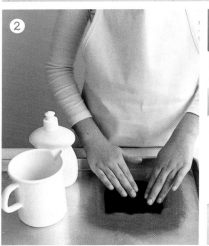

FELTED-WOOL PURSES HOW-TO

SUPPLIES:

- Plastic garbage bag
- Scissors
- Wool roving (unspun wool); available at craft stores
- Rimmed baking sheet
- Liquid soap
- Small pitcher
- Sponge
- Washboard
- Bamboo mat
- Rubber bands
- Needle and thread

STEPS:

1. CUT a template from a garbage bag to the size and shape you want your purse to be. PULL off strips of wool about 1½ inches longer than the template is wide. The pieces should be just thick enough to be opaque. LAY the wool in 3 layers, alternating crosswise and lengthwise layers, on a rimmed baking sheet. The pile should squish down to about ¼ inch thick when you press on it.

2. PLACE the template on top of the wool. FILL a pitcher with hot soapy water. FELT the wool: WET the wool under the template, but not the edges, with the water. TAP firmly through the template for about 10 minutes. (SOP up excess water with a sponge and squeeze back into pitcher as you work.)

3. To "hem" the opening of the purse, WET top edge; FOLD it under the template, and FELT it (repeat wetting and tapping). FOLD remaining edges up over the template; FELT them, and the rest of the purse, for 2 to 3 minutes.

4. BUILD another layer in the same manner (see step 1); LAY it on top of the template. (The template stays in place to keep the two sides from felting together.) WET the wool; tap with your fingers for about 10 minutes. FLIP purse; CREATE a hem as before. FOLD edges of your new layer up over purse; FELT them together.

5. ADD decorations, like stripes, dots, flower shapes, or other simple images, with strips or other pieces of wool in other colors. WORK for about 15 minutes more per side, keeping wool wet and warm as you work.

6. When the felt feels like it will not fall apart, REMOVE template, STICK your hand in the purse, and RUB it on the washboard (also known as "fulling"). MOVE only a tiny bit and CHANGE directions every few strokes, since felt shrinks in the direction you rub. USE slightly longer strokes as the felt strengthens. Be sure to RUB (or "full") all edges.

7. For a handle, ROLL fleece between your palms to form a snake as long as the handle you want. DIP in hot soapy water. ROLL it inside a bamboo mat a little bit, then ADD more fleece. REROLL inside mat; SECURE mat with rubber bands. ROLL back and forth for about 15 minutes, until handle is hardened. When dry, ATTACH to purse by hand sewing with needle and thread.

BEASTLY MITTENS

Everyone—mitten lovers and objectors alike—should fall for these adorable accessories, designed to look like ferocious creatures. Stitch felt features like scales, fins, and a hairy mane onto fleece mittens, then attach facial details like beady eyes, pointy teeth, and flaring nostrils.

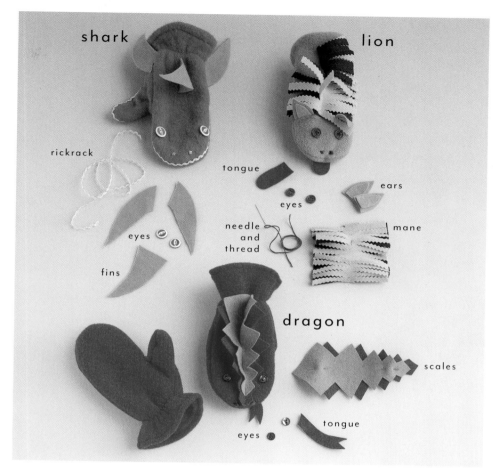

SUPPLIES:

- Beastly Mittens templates (see page 333)
- Fleece mittens
- Felt, in various colors to coordinate with the mittens
- Scissors and pinking shears
- Needle and thread
- Buttons, embroidery floss, and rickrack, for details
- Iron
- Straight pins
- White craft glue

to make shark mittens

Use templates to cut out 3 light-blue felt fins for each mitten (ours are teal blue); sew one on each side of mitten and one on top. For teeth, stitch a length of tiny white rickrack to front curve of mitten. Sew buttons on for eyes. Embroider 2 dots for nostrils (see page 144 for basic instructions).

to make lion mittens

Use templates to cut out all pieces: For mane, cut 2 wide felt pieces (one black, one gold) to cover the top three-quarters of each mitten. An adult should crease felt lengthwise down the middle with an iron. Pin pieces together, and then cut a fringe on each side with pinking shears. Stack pieces and sew to top of mitten along the crease. Glue pink and orange felt triangles together for ears, and sew on; cut a felt tongue, and sew onto underside of mitten. Sew buttons on for eyes, and embroider dots for nostrils (see page 144).

to make dragon mittens

For each mitten, use templates to cut out 2 same-shape felt pieces in 2 colors for scales. Stack; slide top piece down slightly. Pin together; an adult should crease down the middle with an iron, and sew to mitten along crease. Sew on a notched red felt rectangle for a darting tongue. Sew buttons on for eyes, and embroider dots for nostrils (see page 144).

BUTTON
BRACELETS

A box of buttons can inspire
hours of jewelry making. String
them on elastic cord to make
stretchy bracelets. Shank
buttons (with smooth faces)
overlap naturally, while standard
buttons, strung through holes
in their centers, should lie flat.

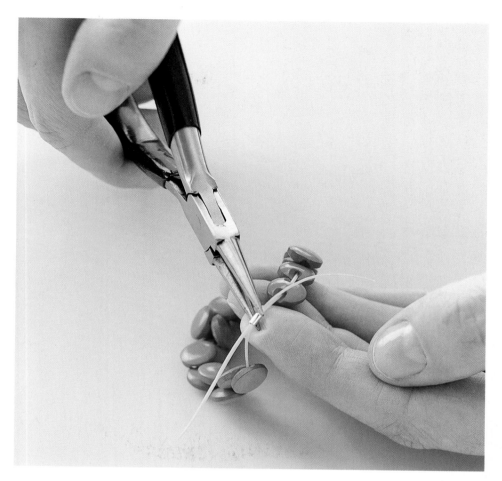

SUPPLIES:

· Elasticized cord
· Scissors
· Buttons
· Metal crimp tube (available in beading and crafts shops)
· Pliers

STEPS:

1. CUT elasticized cord long enough to wrap around the wrist twice.

2. To make a standard-button bracelet, THREAD elastic through from back to front and then to the back again. For 4-hole buttons, THREAD elastic diagonally through 2 holes on opposite corners.

3. For a shank-button bracelet, THREAD elastic through shanks, turning every other button upside down to overlap (as shown).

4. Once you've strung on enough buttons to reach around the wrist, THREAD both ends of elastic through a metal crimp tube and SQUEEZE tightly with pliers. TRIM off excess elastic.

FELT FLOWER BARRETTES

Put a fresh flower behind your ear, and it will last for an hour or two. Make a pair of hairclips adorned with felt blooms, though, and you can enjoy their beauty anytime you like. These barrettes are easy to make in bulk, assembly-line style, so you can create multiple pairs at once.

poppy   pansy   daisy   tulip   clover

SUPPLIES:

- Felt, in various colors
- Felt Flower Barrettes templates (see page 333)
- Scissors
- Low-temperature glue gun
- Bobby pins, in coordinating colors

STEPS:

1. For poppy: CUT a long, narrow strip of felt, ROLL it tightly and GLUE to secure for center. Use the templates to CUT out petal and leaf shapes in contrasting colors. GLUE leaf to back of petal and coiled center to front, LET dry, then GLUE flower to bobby pin.

2. For pansy: Make flower center by cutting a long rectangle of felt into fringe; ROLL it tightly and GLUE along bottom edge to secure. Use the template to CUT out petal shape in a contrasting color. GLUE center to petal, LET dry, then PINCH the petals to form a cup shape and GLUE onto bobby pin.

3. For daisy: CUT a long, narrow strip of felt, ROLL it tightly and GLUE to secure for center. Use the template to CUT four sets of 2 petals in contrasting colors. PINCH petal ends together and GLUE pairs to bobby pin; GLUE on center.

4. For tulip: Use the template to CUT out tulip and leaf shapes in contrasting colors. PINCH at bottom to create a cupped shape, and GLUE to secure, then GLUE flower and leaf to bobby pin. Alternately, LEAVE tulip flat and GLUE to bobby pin.

5. For four-leaf clover: Use the template to CUT out 4 clover shapes. PINCH each leaf at the bottom to cup, and GLUE to secure. GLUE leaves to bobby pin.

FRIENDSHIP BRACELETS

Patterned bracelets woven from embroidery floss are fun to make and to share. Once you learn the basic technique, you can expand your repertoire to include a range of stylish necklaces and even belts (use yarn instead of floss).

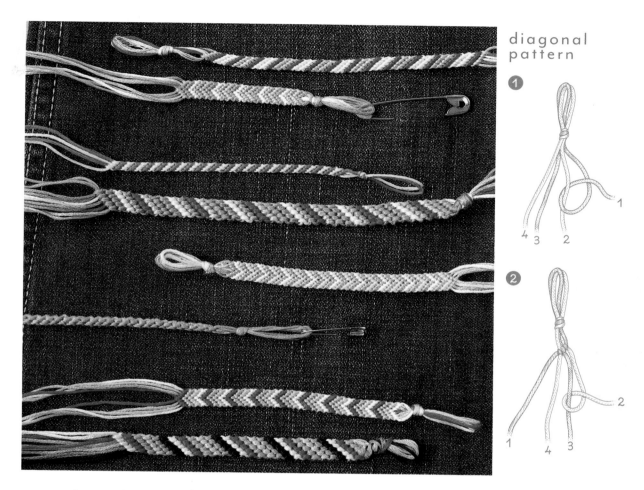

diagonal pattern

1

2

to make a diagonal pattern

Start with two 56-inch threads; if you use more than 2, use longer threads. The more threads you use of the same color, the thicker the stripes. To begin, fold threads in half and knot at folded end, leaving a loop. You now have 4 strings. Follow illustrations (above right) to create the pattern.

1. Loop string 1 around 2 as shown, pulling knot tight toward top. Repeat. Then use string 1 to make 2 knots each on strings 3 and 4.

2. Now string 1 will be on the other side. Repeat same steps with string 2. Row 3 will start with string 3. Continue until bracelet is desired length. To fasten, divide ends in half; tie together through loop.

to make a chevron pattern

To create this design with 4 threads, fold and knot so you have 8 strings. Arrange strings so colors mirror each other (for example, make strings 1 and 8 blue; 2 and 7 red; and so on). Starting from the outside, knot string 1 to string 2 (tying twice as described, left), then knot string 1 to strings 3 and 4. Next, knot string 8 to strings 7, 6, and 5. Last, knot string 1 to string 8 in the middle. Then repeat for next row. Continue until bracelet is desired length. To fasten, tie ends together through loop.

CLAY BEAD JEWELRY

When it's molded, pierced, and baked, polymer clay can be fashioned into baubles, ready for stringing into colorful jewelry. Combine balls, disks, and strings to create unique designs, and then thread the beads onto string for necklaces and onto cord for bracelets.

cute as a button

Instead of forming into balls, press the polymer clay to flatten, then use a plastic knife or small cookie cutter to cut the clay into round button shapes. Poke holes with a toothpick before baking.

tips

For the projects here, start by making a bunch of solid polymer clay balls, then adorn them with dots, swirls, flowers, and faces.

- Whatever you're shaping, you'll need to make the clay soft and pliable. When a new package is opened, the clay may feel hard or crumbly—just knead it and roll it in your hands.

- Be sure your hands are clean when switching to a different color so the shade doesn't transfer.

- Clay balls can flatten if they're set down. To prevent this, use a paper-clip skewer: Straighten a paper clip; slide balls onto it, leaving space in between so they're not touching one another. Balance the skewer across the top of a cup. (You will use the holes to string the baked beads onto cord or string.)

- Bake the beads, on their skewers, in the oven at 275°F (use an oven thermometer for accuracy) 6 to 15 minutes, or according to package directions. (Baking time varies according to size of bead; bake in batches of similar size for best results.) If the clay hasn't hardened after it cools, bake it for a few minutes more.

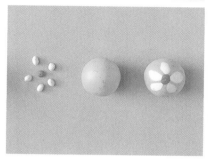

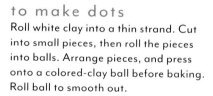

to make dots

Roll white clay into a thin strand. Cut into small pieces, then roll the pieces into balls. Arrange pieces, and press onto a colored-clay ball before baking. Roll ball to smooth out.

to make daisies

For the petals, make 5 small white clay balls; make a small orange ball to use as the center of the flower. Arrange pieces, and press onto a colored-clay ball. Roll ball to smooth out before baking.

to make faces

Roll a small piece of clay into a ball; with your thumb, flatten into a disk. Make tiny clay balls for eyes and nose and a tiny log for mouth. Arrange pieces on a disk, and press the assembled face onto a clay ball. Roll ball to smooth out before baking.

to make swirls

Roll white clay into a thin strand, wrap around a colored-clay ball, and press. Roll ball to smooth out before baking.

ORIGAMI RINGS

These oversize paper "gems" are as much fun to make as they are to wear. Craft them as a party activity, then send the reveler home with his or her own handiwork.

HOW-TO

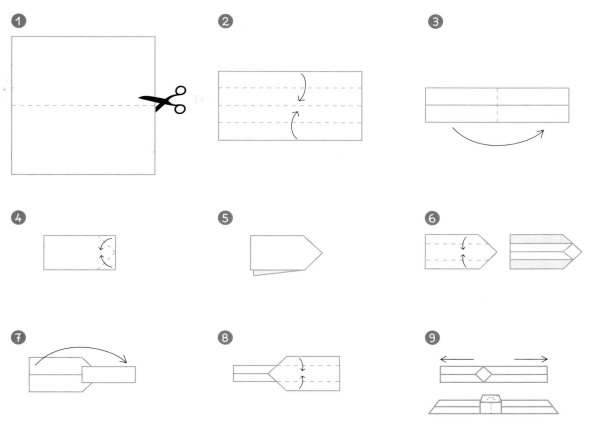

STEPS:

1. CUT origami paper in half.

2. FOLD in half lengthwise (right side down). UNFOLD, then fold top and bottom parts to meet at center.

3. FOLD paper in half from left to right.

4. FOLD the right corners toward you to meet at the center and unfold. Then fold the same corners away from you in the same manner; UNFOLD.

5. TUCK corners inside folded paper along the creases.

6. FOLD upper and lower edges of top layer to meet at the center.

7. FOLD this central piece to the right; FLIP paper over.

8. FOLD upper and lower edges of the flip side to meet at the center.

9. PULL ends to open center box; use fingers to flatten and shape top of box. GLUE or TAPE the right and left parts together to complete the ring, trimming ends as needed.

PAPER BEAD NECKLACE

The bright beads on these necklaces are so artful, no one will ever guess how easy they are to make. Each bead is made by rolling slim triangles of paper around a toothpick. We used origami paper, but wrapping paper or clippings from a magazine would also work beautifully.

SUPPLIES:

- Origami paper (or other decorative paper), in 4-by-4-inch squares
- Pencil
- Ruler
- Scissors
- Toothpicks
- White craft glue
- Small paintbrush
- String

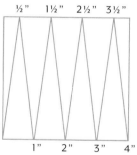

STEPS:

1. Each 4-by-4-inch square will make seven 1-inch beads. On one edge of each square, MARK a point at 1-inch intervals. On the opposite side, MARK points at ½ inch, 1½ inches, 2½ inches, and 3½ inches. USE a ruler to connect the marks, making diagonal lines. These lines create 7 triangles: 4 pointing one way and 3 pointing the other. CUT out triangles.

2. For each triangle, PLACE colored side of paper facedown. PLACE a toothpick that's a bit longer than the base of the triangle on the wide end, and ROLL the paper around the toothpick tightly for about ½ inch. SPREAD glue along the rest of the triangle with a paintbrush, then finish rolling until the end. SLIDE bead off the toothpick, and LET dry.

3. CUT a piece of string to desired length of necklace, and knot 1 inch from the end. SLIP the beads onto the string; TIE ends together, and TRIM.

BEADED FLOWER JEWELRY

You can wear a daisy chain all year long when you make one from dainty seed beads. And you can cast them in whatever color combinations you like best—from the prettiest pastels to the brightest bolds.

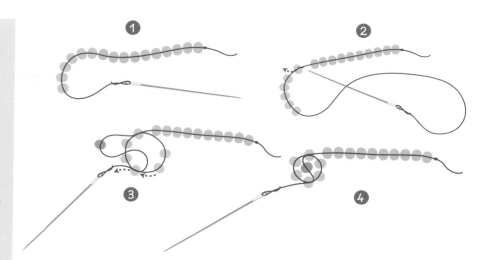

beading tips

- **Choose your beads:** Round seed beads are available in different sizes at crafts stores and bead shops, online, and from mail-order catalogs.

- **Select your stringing material:** We like coated wire, which comes in many colors. It's strong and flexible, so you can string beads along it without a needle. Elastic cord is a good choice for jewelry, but you'll need to use a beading needle with it. Keep your bead size in mind when choosing a stringing material—whatever you choose must be able to pass through the bead's hole twice.

- **Prepare your work surface:** Sit in a nice bright spot, near a window or a lamp. Cover a tray or table with felt or other fabric to stop beads from rolling, and keep beads separated by color in shallow dishes or jar lids.

- **Pick up beads properly:** Beads can be hard to pick up with fingers. Before you know it, they're bouncing all over the floor. To avoid this, lift beads by poking the end of your wire or tip of your needle into the hole, then use your fingers to slide the bead up the wire.

STEPS:

1. To make daisy chains, first SNIP a piece of elastic cord four times the length you want your finished item to be; THREAD one end through a clasp, and TIE a double knot. THREAD the other end through a needle (use a needle threader) but don't tie a knot; LEAVE a 2-inch tail instead. SLIP a few seed beads onto the cord to start the chain. To add a flower, STRING six beads onto the cord.

2. SLIP needle through first flower bead again (the needle should point away from knotted end).

3. To make the center of the daisy, SLIP one bead onto the cord, then PASS the needle through the fourth flower bead in the opposite direction.

4. PULL tight to create daisy. To add a leaf, SLIP 10 to 12 beads onto the end of the cord. LOOP the cord, then PASS the end back through the first leaf bead. TUG on cord until beads are snug. Then continue to bead the rest of the piece.

5. PULL tight. To end bracelets and necklaces, SLIP on a few beads, then TIE on a clasp (or just TIE ends). To end rings, THREAD the cord back through a few beads.

SUPPLIES:

- Scissors
- Elastic cord (0.5-mm gauge)
- Clasps
- Beading needle
- Needle threader
- Seed beads in assorted colors (2.5- to 3-mm size)

TIE-DYE T-SHIRTS

Groovy patterns are so much fun—and so easy—to create. The instructions on the next few pages produce three popular designs, but feel free to experiment to make patterns of your own—the possibilities are endless. For best results, use T-shirts made of 100 percent cotton.

did you know?
Tie-dyeing is a "resist" technique: Fabric is cinched so that when it's immersed, only certain areas are dyed. The undyed parts form decorative patterns.

SUPPLIES:

· Cotton T-shirts
· Rubber bands
· Rubber gloves
· Fabric dye
· Large nonreactive
  bowl, such as glass
  or enamel
· Salt (optional)
· Spoon
· Marbles
· Mild detergent
· Clean old towel
· Clothespins

BASIC STEPS:

1. To begin, CHOOSE a pattern and tie fabric accordingly with rubber bands (see specific pattern instructions on the following 2 pages). Wearing rubber gloves to protect your hands from stains, MIX dye in large bowl following manufacturer's instructions. If desired, ADD a cup of salt to deepen the color.

2. IMMERSE a garment in dye and gently SWISH it around with a spoon. REMOVE when the color looks slightly darker than you want; this should take 5 to 20 minutes. RINSE the fabric in warm water and then in cool water until water runs clear.

3. REMOVE rubber bands. HAND-WASH T-shirt with a mild detergent and warm water, and RINSE with cool water (or LAUNDER it by itself in a washing machine). WRING T-shirt in a clean old towel and then line-dry, or machine-dry on the coolest setting.

TIE-DYE T-SHIRTS HOW-TO

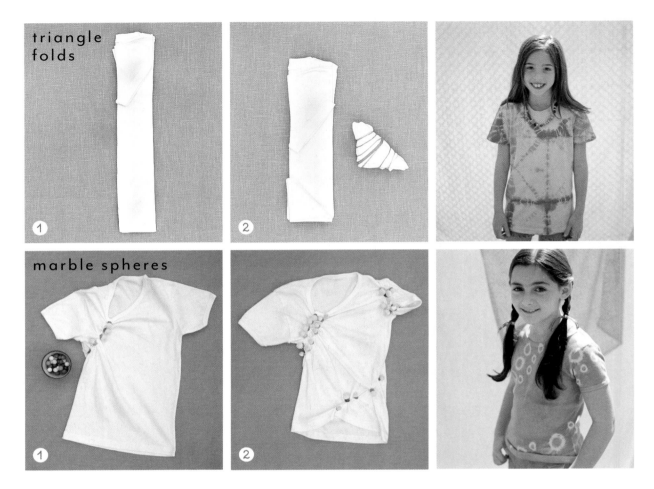

triangle folds

marble spheres

to make triangle folds

1. FOLD T-shirt in half lengthwise twice; FOLD sleeves so they're facing outward.

2. FOLD up bottom corner of fabric at a 90-degree angle, and REPEAT until you are left with a triangle of fabric. BIND T-shirt with rubber bands. Tie-dye according to instructions on page 191.

to make marble spheres

1. DECIDE on a layout for your pattern. LAY a marble inside the flat T-shirt, and CINCH fabric over it with a rubber band.

2. REPEAT with additional marbles to complete your desired pattern. Tie-dye according to instructions on page 191.

pleated stripes

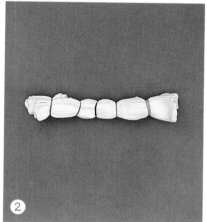

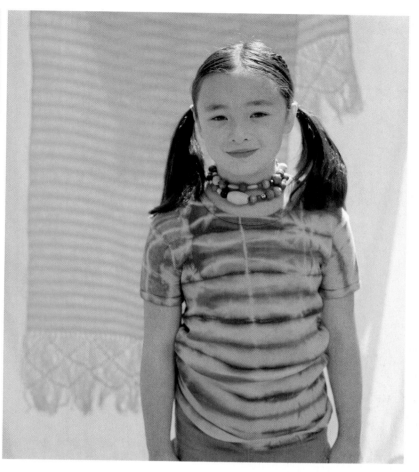

to make pleated stripes

1. LAY T-shirt flat, and FOLD in its sleeves.
   ACCORDION-FOLD the shirt from the bottom
   up in the desired stripe width.

2. CINCH one end of the folded shirt with a
   rubber band; REPEAT every inch or so. Tie-dye
   according to instructions on page 191.

SUPERHERO COSTUMES

Zap! Kapow! Wham! Small—but nonetheless strong—superheroes are ready at
a moment's notice to jump into some crime-fighting action. Luckily, with a little help from
a grown-up, any kid can whip up a costume lickety-split. Start with leggings and
long-sleeve T-shirts, and then customize with capes, utility belts, masks, and initials to
hint at the well-guarded wearers' heroic abilities. Instructions for the belt, cuffs, and
mask are on the following pages.

CAPE AND T-SHIRT HOW-TO

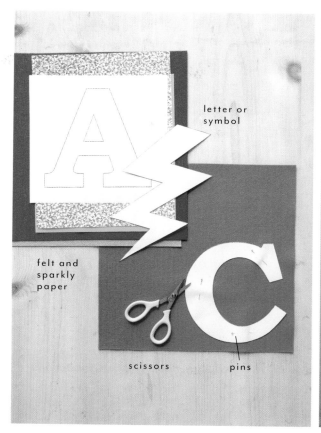

letter or symbol

felt and sparkly paper

scissors

pins

polyester satin

ribbon

fabric glue

T-shirt

SUPPLIES:

- Small sharp scissors
- Superhero Costumes templates (see pages 334 and 335)
- Disappearing-ink fabric pen
- Felt and art papers (including glitter papers)
- 36-by-36-inch piece of polyester satin
- Iron
- T-shirt
- Needle and thread or sewing machine and basic sewing supplies, including safety pin
- 24 inches of ½-inch-wide ribbon
- Fabric glue

to make a cape and t-shirt

1. CUT out the letter or lightning symbol template. TRACE onto felt or art paper with a disappearing-ink pen, and CUT out.

2. Make cape: FOLD over one side of the satin fabric by 1 inch, and PRESS with a cool iron (an adult should do the ironing). SEW down flap, creating a channel. ATTACH safety pin to one end of ribbon, and THREAD through.

3. ATTACH letter or symbol: LAY cape or T-shirt flat. SPREAD glue all over the back of the letter or symbol, and POSITION on cape or shirt. LET dry.

SUPERHERO COSTUMES HOW-TO

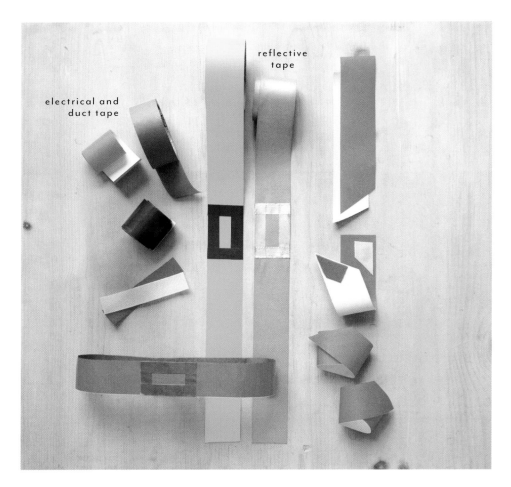

electrical and
duct tape

reflective
tape

SUPPLIES:

- **2-inch-wide strip of kraft paper (cut to fit around child's waist with 1-inch overlap)**
- **Electrical, duct, painter's, or reflective tape, in a variety of colors**
- **Superhero Costumes templates (see page 335)**
- **Small sharp scissors**
- **Pen**
- **Two 2-by-8-inch strips of kraft paper or muslin**

to make a belt and cuffs

1. Make belt: COVER long paper strip with desired tape. To create belt buckle, TRIM pieces of tape and STICK them to the center of strip. Wrap belt around child's body and tape in place (or secure with glue).

2. Make cuffs: TRACE template onto the shorter strips of paper, and CUT out. COVER cutout with desired tape. WRAP around wrist so the ends overlap at a slight angle, forming a peak. TAPE in place.

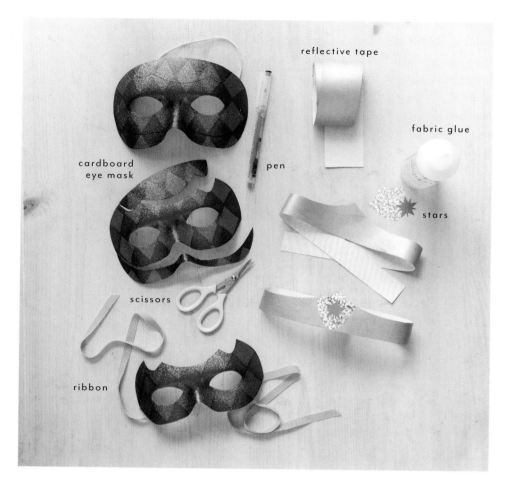

reflective tape

fabric glue

cardboard
eye mask

pen

stars

scissors

ribbon

SUPPLIES:

- Cardboard eye mask
- Pen
- Small sharp scissors
- Fabric glue
- Two 10-inch pieces of ½-inch-wide ribbon
- Superhero Costumes templates (see page 335)
- Reflective tape
- 2-inch-wide strip of kraft paper (cut to fit around child's head with 1-inch overlap)
- Glitter paper
- Cut-out or punched paper stars

to make a mask and headband

1. To customize mask, use a pen to DRAW your desired outline, and TRIM along marked lines. (SNIP from top and bottom, but leave sides intact.) REMOVE the mask's elastic, and GLUE ribbon at sides.

2. Make headband: AFFIX paper strip to reflective tape, then TRACE headband template onto paper side and cut out. TRACE crest template onto glitter paper; CUT out. GLUE star to crest, then GLUE crest to headband. LET dry. CENTER crest on forehead, and WRAP band around head; GLUE ends.

FOIL-AND-PAPER CROWNS

Some occasions call for the royal treatment. Whether you need extra-special party hats for your next bash or just want the perfect accent for day-to-day dress-up wear, a sparkling crown fits the bill. You can make this version with materials you probably already have at home.

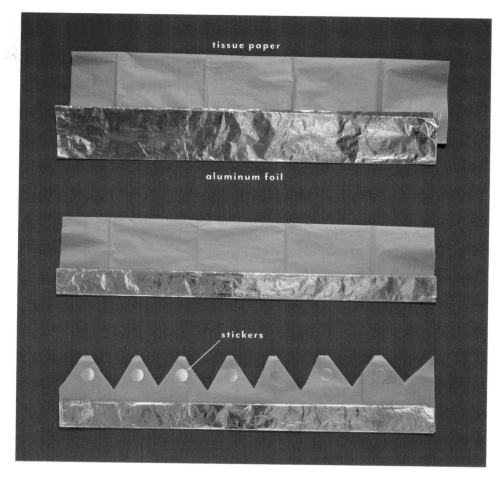

tissue paper

aluminum foil

stickers

SUPPLIES:

· Aluminum foil
· Colored tissue paper
· Scissors
· Dot stickers
· Tape or stapler

STEPS:

1. TEAR off a piece of aluminum foil 20 inches long. FOLD in half twice, long sides together, for cuff; LAY cuff with opening toward top. FOLD 20-inch-wide tissue paper in half lengthwise twice; SLIP inside V of cuff, folded edge up, so bottom edge is just below center of cuff.

2. FOLD foil strip in half again, folding up from the bottom (this will hold the tissue in place).

3. CUT V's in tissue paper, leaving attached at the fold, and DECORATE with stickers. OVERLAP ends to proper size, and SLIP one end of foil inside the other. TAPE or STAPLE in place.

TRICKED-OUT SHOELACES

Why tie shoes the same old way when creative crisscrossing will brighten the day? These shoe-lacing methods keep shoes snug and secure while looking super rad.

all tied up

Bye-bye, boring white laces. Buy a couple of pairs in bright hues to complement your kicks (or if you want to get really wild, try shoes in two different colors, too), then experiment with different weaves and loops to create fun patterns. Here are four of our faves.

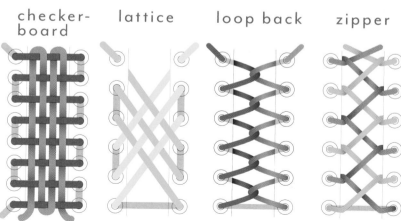

checker-board **lattice** **loop back** **zipper**

EMBELLISHED FLIP-FLOPS

Here's a quick, fun, foolproof way to dress up even the most plain-Jane rubber sandals. A butterfly fluttering near your toes is pretty; a slithering snake or spotted lizard might just make your friends jump out of their suits!

flip-flops

plastic animals and insects

glue gun

tip ✳
Tubes filled with plastic animals or insects can be found in many toy stores but also at the gift shops of zoos and natural history museums. Make sure the bottom of the figure has a flat surface so it will adhere to the strap of the shoe.

SUPPLIES:

· Rubber flip-flops
· Plastic animals or insects
· Hot glue gun or Magna-Tac

STEPS:

1. PLAY around with the arrangement of the animals until you like the look; we embellished each flip-flop with only one figure but you can USE as many as you like.

2. An adult should HOT GLUE the creature in place (make sure glue gun is on a high setting). Alternatively, ADHERE with a thick, clear-drying glue, such as Magna-Tac. LET dry before wearing.

POTATO PRINTS

Adding a playful print to a basic T-shirt is as simple as slicing a potato. Thanks to their firm texture, raw potatoes can be easily shaped into stamps, and their smooth interiors take well to being coated with fabric paint (be sure to use a different stamp for each color). You can use cookie cutters or other kitchen molds to turn a spud into a stamp quickly. Ask an adult to cut out shapes and small details with a paring knife.

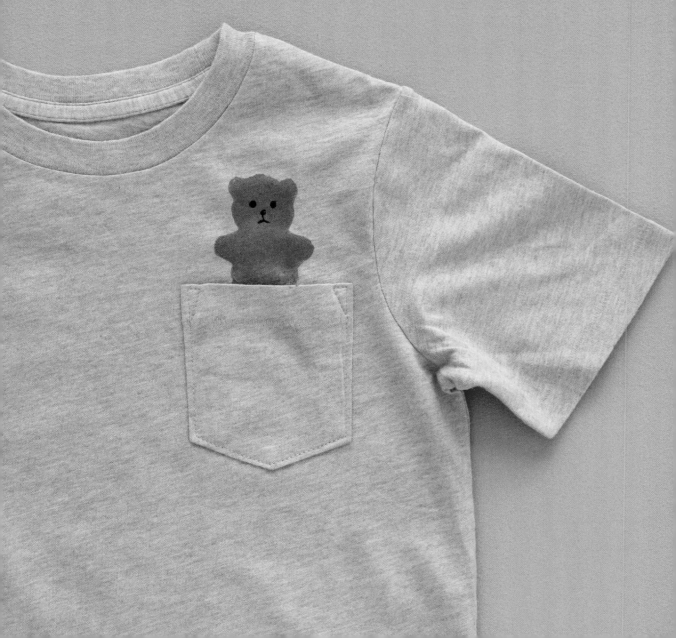

HOW-TO

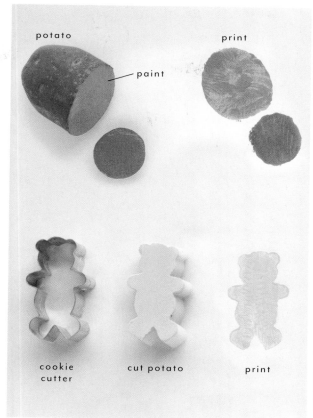

potato · paint · print

cookie cutter · cut potato · print

SUPPLIES:

- Sharp knife
- Potatoes (we used a large russet)
- Cookie cutters
- Paper towels
- Fabric paint and paintbrushes
- Paper plate
- Craft stick
- Cotton T-shirt
- Cardboard

STEPS:

1. An adult should SLICE a potato in half lengthwise. To make the flower, we used a larger, oval-shaped potato to stamp the petals and a smaller round potato for the flower's center.

2. For the bear, PLACE cookie cutter on cut side of one half; SET aside other potato half to use for another stamp. PUSH cutter through potato, keeping potato flat on table; BREAK away excess potato. POKE shape out of cutter; BLOT away any moisture with a paper towel.

3. SPREAD a thin layer of fabric paint on a paper plate using a craft stick. DIP shape into paint a few times, moving it around for an even coat; WIPE off any paint on sides of stamp with a paper towel.

4. STAMP shape onto the T-shirt (SLIP cardboard inside shirt first), pressing down firmly for 5 seconds. Paint details such as flower stem and bear's facial features. LET set according to paint manufacturer's instructions.

FISH PRINT T-SHIRT

Everything will go just swimmingly when you're wearing this aquatic-themed tee. Using fabric paint and a rubber fish, it couldn't be easier to give your outfit a splashy update.

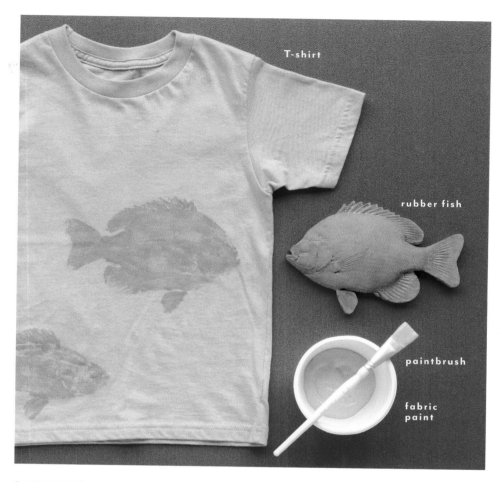

T-shirt

rubber fish

paintbrush

fabric
paint

SUPPLIES:

· Fabric paint and
  paintbrush
· Rubber fish
· Cotton T-shirt

STEPS:

1. If desired, MIX paints to find a shade that suits the
   fabric. BRUSH a thin layer of fabric paint onto
   rubber fish, making sure to cover all the textures
   of the surface.

2. PLACE fish on work surface. LAY shirt over fish
   and, with fingers, press thoroughly all over to
   pick up the details (but be careful not to shift the
   mold). Carefully LIFT shirt up. LET set according
   to paint manufacturer's instructions.

CHAPTER 5

EXPERIMENT AND EXPLORE

There's no end to the fun you can have when you engage with the wonders of the natural world around you.

MONSTER SALT CRYSTALS

Growing tiny salt crystals into gigantic ones is fascinating to observe and record. You'll need patience for this project—it takes several days, but it's well worth it.

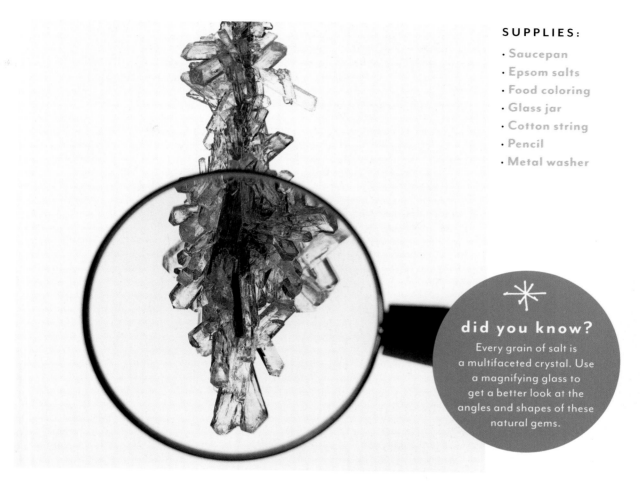

did you know?

Every grain of salt is a multifaceted crystal. Use a magnifying glass to get a better look at the angles and shapes of these natural gems.

STEPS:

1. POUR 1 cup water into a saucepan. An adult should bring water to a boil, then REMOVE from heat. ADD ½ cup of Epsom salts and stir until it dissolves; if you like, ADD a few drops of food coloring. Keep adding salt until it no longer dissolves when stirred (¼ to ½ cup more). LET cool, and then POUR the mixture into a glass jar.

2. TIE a cotton string to the center of a pencil, and TIE a metal washer to the other end of the string; the string should be long enough so the washer hangs a couple of inches above the bottom of the jar. SET pencil on jar with washer dangling inside. WATCH over the next few days (BREAK away any crust that forms at the top of the jar): As the water evaporates, the salt left behind will join together, forming large crystals.

3. KEEP your salt formation on display after the water is gone: REMOVE the salt-covered string and hang it in a clean jar.

WATER FIREWORKS

Set off an explosion—of color, that is. These spectacular bursts are made in a water-filled jar using basic kitchen ingredients. Fill a clear jar with water. In a separate cup, combine 1 tablespoon vegetable oil and a few drops each of red, blue, and yellow liquid food coloring; mix them together with a fork. Pour the colored oil into the jar of water, and watch as streamers of color descend.

did you know?

Food coloring is water-soluble: It cannot dissolve in oil, only in water. When you first pour the mixture into the jar, the food coloring is trapped in the oil; eventually it sinks, makes contact with the water, and dissolves.

GLASS JAR XYLOPHONE

Music is an art, to be sure, but it's also a science—the science of sound. To appreciate how sounds are formed, make a xylophone by filling a group of jars with water. To begin, fill jars with varying levels of water (stir in some food coloring for a prettier presentation). You'll see that leaving different amounts of empty space at the top creates a range of notes when you tap out a tune with a spare drumstick or mallet.

did you know?

In percussion, you hit, strike, or shake a hollow instrument and the vibrations, called *sound waves*, bounce around inside and get louder. The earliest percussion instruments were probably hollow logs. Modern-day versions include drums, tambourines, maracas, castanets, cymbals, and xylophones.

GIANT BUBBLE WAND

When it comes to bubble-making contests, those wands that come in little plastic bottles just don't do the job. Luckily, it's easy to create a blower that produces oversize bubbles—and a homemade solution that will keep you in steady supply.

did you know?

A bubble is made of a thin film of soap formed around a pocket of air. The dishwashing soap in bubble solution makes the water become flexible, and the force of surface tension allows the solution to hold the shape of a bubble when air is blown into it. Regardless of a bubble's initial shape, it will try to become a sphere.

SUPPLIES:

- Liquid dishwashing soap
- Light corn syrup
- Large shallow container
- Cotton twine
- Drinking straws
- Bubble solution
- Scissors

STEPS:

1. To make bubble solution, POUR 10 cups water, 4 cups dishwashing soap, and 1 cup corn syrup into a large shallow container. STIR to combine. (You can also use store-bought solution.)

2. THREAD cotton twine through 2 straws (CUT off any flexible section of the straws), and MAKE a rectangle with straws as long sides and string for short sides (see opposite); KNOT, and TRIM excess.

3. Holding straws, and keeping blower slack, DIP in solution and lift out. Then carefully PULL straws apart so string is tight, and BLOW (you may need to practice a bit). You can CHANGE position of straws to form bubbles of different shapes and sizes. For the wand shown above right, simply SHIFT the straws so they are end to end on the bottom with string on top.

WEATHER WATCHING

Ah, the beauty of a blustery day. Not only is it great for flying a kite, but it can also teach you a few things about weather forecasting. Meteorologists measure wind speed and direction to help estimate what the day will be like. You can give it a try with a few simple handmade tools.

did you know?

Calculate wind speed: In this windmill-like device, called an **anemometer**, the breeze catches the cups and sends them spinning, helping you calculate wind speed. Count its rotations to determine how fast the wind is blowing. Take care with the measurements; precision will help you get an accurate result.

ANEMOMETER HOW-TO

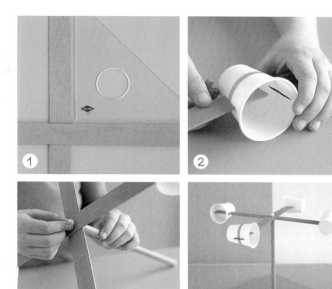

SUPPLIES:

- Acrylic paint and paintbrush
- 8-inch wooden square, for base
- ½-inch wooden dowel (10 inches long)
- Two 14-by-1-inch balsa-wood slats
- Pushpins
- Wood glue
- T-square or right angle
- Utility knife
- 4 paper cups
- Colored tape
- Map tacks
- Drill

STEPS:

1. USE acrylic paint to COAT the wooden base, dowel, and balsa-wood slats. With a pushpin, MAKE a hole through the exact center of each slat. DAB glue around top center of one slat; PLACE other slat on top, and make slats perpendicular with the T-square or right angle. LET glue dry. INSERT pushpin through both holes.

2. In each of the paper cups, an adult should use a utility knife to CUT two 1½-inch-long slits on opposite sides. MARK one cup with tape. SLIDE each cup over a slat so cups all face the same way.

3. PLACE crossed slats on top of the dowel; MAKE a hole in the dowel with pushpin. REPLACE pushpin with map tack, making sure slats spin freely. An adult should DRILL a ½-inch hole in the base. DAB glue in hole; insert the dowel; LET dry.

4. To calculate wind speed in miles per hour, COUNT number of rotations (how many times the marked cup passes the same point) in 10 seconds, then DIVIDE by 4.

WIND VANE HOW-TO

SUPPLIES:

- Acrylic paint and paintbrush
- 8-inch wooden square, for base
- ½-inch wooden dowel (10 inches long)
- Small letter stencils or stickers
- Drill
- Wood glue
- Pencil
- Wind Vane Bird template (see page 335)
- Orange vinyl
- Scissors
- Clear glue
- Pushpin
- Map tack
- Compass

STEPS:

1. USE acrylic paint to COAT the wooden base and dowel. LET dry. USE stencils to paint N, E, S, and W on base (or attach stickers). An adult should DRILL a ½-inch hole in center of base. DAB glue in hole; insert dowel, and LET dry.

2. TRACE bird template onto vinyl; CUT out. CREASE at fold lines and then glue tabs on bottom together. With pushpin, MAKE centered hole in top of dowel. BALANCE bird on dowel; PUSH map tack through hole, making sure bird spins freely.

3. PLACE base so that N faces north using a compass. The vane will point to the direction the wind is coming from.

CORNSTARCH QUICKSAND

This strange, shape-shifting goop feels otherworldly. Try to hold it in your hand and it'll ooze through your fingers; punch it, though, and suddenly the surface is hard. What's going on? Made with cornstarch and water, this quicksand-like mixture is called a hydrosol, a solid scattered throughout a liquid, and it has the properties of both at once.

SUPPLIES:

· Bowl
· Cornstarch
· Water

STEPS:

1. In a bowl, COMBINE 1 cup cornstarch with ½ cup water, and STIR with your fingers until mixture is a thick paste; if the mixture is too crumbly, ADD 1 tablespoon water. (WASH hands afterward.)

2. PUNCH the surface: Your fist will barely make a dent. Now slowly DIP your hand into it. You can PICK it up, and it will ooze through your fingers. SQUEEZE it, TURN it over and over in your hands, and WATCH how it goes from goopy liquid to dry powder and back to glop.

NATURAL GAS EXPERIMENT

With some very ordinary ingredients, you can easily inflate a balloon—without any huffing and puffing. It works because of the chemical reaction between baking soda and vinegar, which creates carbon dioxide. This gas fills the bottle and can't escape, so it rushes into the balloon.

GAS

 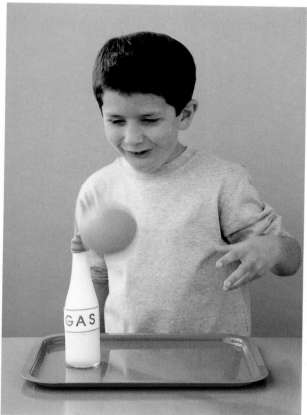

SUPPLIES:

- Vinegar
- Clean glass bottle
- Funnel
- Small balloon
- Baking soda

STEPS:

1. POUR ¼ cup of vinegar into the glass bottle.

2. USE a funnel to FILL a small balloon with 1 tablespoon of baking soda.

3. Holding the balloon so that the bulb falls to one side, carefully SLIP the mouth of the balloon over the neck of the bottle.

4. Then LIFT the bulb to let the baking soda fall into the bottle. LET go and watch as the balloon inflates all by itself!

SOLAR SYSTEM BEDROOM

Any kid who dreams of visiting the distant reaches of our solar system will delight in gazing at the cosmos from his or her very own bed. Create models of each planet (and the sun) and hang each from the ceiling using adhesive hooks and monofilament (or string). Map out the stars on a window shade for a private planetarium show.

did you know?

Though only a medium-size star, the **sun** is large enough to fit a million Earths inside.

to make the twinkling shade

Start with a midnight-blue roll-up shade; then print out a diagram of the constellations Orion and Taurus (or other constellations) from a copyright-free source on the Internet, enlarging as necessary to fit shade. Place the enlarged copy on top of the shade with a piece of cardboard underneath to protect your work surface, and punch holes through both paper and shade with a screw punch. Choose a small punch for distant (dimmer) stars, a larger one for closer (brighter) stars. Connect the dots with a white gel paint pen.

to make the sun

Working over a well-protected surface, splatter-paint sunspots onto a yellow paper lantern: Dip an old toothbrush into water, then into red and orange paint; pull thumb through bristles, flicking paint onto lantern.

SOLAR SYSTEM BEDROOM HOW-TO

saturn

did you know?

Sparkling with rings and surrounded by cold, fast-moving clouds, **Saturn** is visible to the naked eye on a clear night, and moves slowly across the sky.

to make saturn

Ask an adult to cut a hollow 8-inch smooth-surfaced Styrofoam ball (available at crafts stores) into halves with a serrated knife; center one half on a vinyl record album. Mark outside edge of ball onto record; set ball aside. Paint rings of glue around outside edge of record, sprinkling each with a different color glitter. Paint ball halves with wavy stripes in red, yellow, and brown. Punch a hole through top of each ball half using a skewer; string a long piece of monofilament (for hanging) through one hole and hole in record, and tie around a toothpick to anchor underneath record. An adult should hot-glue ball halves to album.

mercury

earth

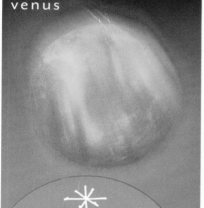
venus

did you know?
Mercury is extremely hot on the side facing the sun, and extremely cold on the side facing away. Because it orbits quickly, this small, rocky planet was named for the Roman messenger God.

did you know?
Our home planet is the only one with liquid water and with the atmospheric conditions to sustain life. **Earth** is also the only planet not named for a Greek or Roman God; the name is derived from the German word for ground.

did you know?
Similar in size to Earth, **Venus** is scorchingly hot and covered in dense sulfuric-acid clouds. One of the brightest planets in the sky, Venus was named for the Roman goddess of love.

to make mercury
Poke a hole in a red rubber SuperBall with an awl, and insert a screw eye into it to hang.

to make venus
Use a yellow tennis ball; its fuzzy surface will make the planet seem to glow. Dip a sponge into red paint, then orange; blot against ball. Attach a screw eye, for hanging.

to make earth
Paint a baseball blue, then blot with a sponge dipped in green paint. Let dry. Brush on white glue in spots for clouds, then sprinkle with white glitter. Use an awl to make a hole for the screw eye, for hanging.

jupiter

uranus

mars

did you know?

When first discovered in 1781, **Uranus** was nearly mistaken for a comet. Glowing faintly blue-green due to its methane atmosphere, it is surrounded by rings of black boulders. It spins on its side, unlike other planets.

did you know?

Mars is about half the size of Earth. Because of evidence that once it had water, scientists believe some life may have existed there. Named for the Roman god of war, Mars is also called the Red Planet because of its rust-colored soil.

to make jupiter

Paint a 10-inch Styrofoam ball (available at crafts stores) with intermittent stripes of white glue; sprinkle with craft sand in brownish and deep orange. Make an elongated oval spot in middle of one side with orange sand, as shown above. To hang, sharpen a long wooden dowel with a pencil sharpener, attach a screw eye to the other end, and insert into the ball.

did you know?

This planet's Great Red Spot is a hurricane that has been in progress at least 100 years. Jupiter is so massive, the Romans named it for their chief god.

to make uranus

Use a 6-inch blue rubber gym ball for the planet. Paint a 6-inch wooden embroidery hoop silver; let dry, brush with glue, and cover with glitter. Tighten hoop vertically around the ball to represent the rings. The hoop's fastener will serve as a hanger.

to make mars

Paint a golf ball red and let dry. An adult should use a drill bit or awl to make a hole; attach a screw eye, for hanging.

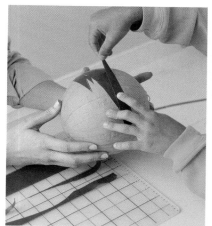

neptune

did you know?

Neptune has a thick atmosphere of methane clouds, which lends it a blue color, and the fastest winds in the solar system. Because it is mostly made up of liquids, the freezing-cold planet was named for the Roman god of the sea.

to make neptune

Start with a 6-inch-diameter papier-mâché ball (available at crafts stores). Have an adult cut thin, wavy strips of blue duct tape with a utility knife; wrap around ball, overlapping, to completely cover. Attach 1 large and 1 small blue dot sticker (from an office-supply store) to represent the planet's dark, stormy spots. Lightly brush with white glue and then glitter for clouds. Attach a screw eye, for hanging.

PRESSED LEAVES

It's no surprise that your pockets are stuffed after a walk in the woods—nature is full of interesting finds around every bend. After collecting a bunch of leaves, preserve them in a homemade leaf press or use them to create rubbings in a journal.

types

edges

colors

shapes

sort it out
It's especially fun to group a growing collection of leaves into categories, such as the ones shown here.

field guide

resealable plastic bag

leaf press

magnifying glass

pencil sharpener

binoculars

colored pencils

field notebook

backpack

compass

SUPPLIES:

- Resealable plastic bag to carry leaves and other finds
- Field guide, for identifying species of trees in the forest
- Paper towels, cardboard, and bungee cord, for the leaf press
- Magnifying glass and binoculars, to inspect specimens up close
- Colored pencils or crayons (and sharpener)
- Notebook and eraser
- Backpack
- Compass

to make a leaf press

Place 2 paper towels on top of 1 piece of cardboard cut the same size as the paper towels. Lay a single layer of leaves on the paper towels, and top with another paper towel. Repeat with remaining leaves. Top last layer of leaves with 2 paper towels and another piece of trimmed cardboard. Secure tightly with a bungee cord. Once home, remove the cord, and place a heavy object on top of press; let sit for at least a week. You may need to change the paper towels after a few days if leaves were wet or freshly fallen.

to make rubbings

Place a leaf (press it first if necessary in a leaf press, above) underneath the paper in your notebook. Make sure it lays flat. With the side of a colored pencil or crayon, rub over the leaf, taking care to capture all the veins and edges. You can also make rubbings of tree bark with the side of a colored pencil or crayon, which results in textured patterns.

SAFARI TERRARIUM

One day, you may very well set off on your own safari adventure. For now, you can get a close-up look at exotic "wildlife" right at home by building a terrarium for toy zebras, giraffes, elephants, and other animals. This environment is completely enclosed, so once you've achieved the right level of moisture, it will almost take care of itself. Good sources for the materials and animals include museum and zoo gift shops, hobby stores, garden centers, and online retailers.

HOW-TO

builder's sand

potting soil

peat moss

charcoal

gravel

SUPPLIES:

- 2½-gallon fish tank
- Gravel
- Finely ground charcoal (available at aquarium stores)
- Potting soil
- Peat moss
- Builder's sand
- Spoon
- Miniature tree, such as Chinese elm
- Grass plants and mist bottle
- Rocks and toy animals
- Acrylic lid for tank (have it cut at a hardware store)

STEPS:

1. COVER the tank bottom with a ¾-inch layer of clean gravel. SCATTER a ¼-inch layer of the ground charcoal on gravel.

2. MIX 2 parts potting soil, 2 parts peat moss, and 1 part builder's sand. PLACE in tank; lightly TAMP down soil. With a spoon, DIG pits just large enough for the plants.

3. REMOVE elm and grass plants from their pots, BRUSH off excess soil, and PLACE in pits. Be careful not to damage the roots, and PLANT them no deeper than they were in their pots. SMOOTH soil gently. ADD rocks and toy animals. PLACE lid on tank. MIST with a spray bottle as needed.

WINDOW GARDEN

What would you trade for a handful of magic beans? As it turns out, all beans—all seeds, for that matter—are magical in their own way. If you don't believe it, just plant one and watch it germinate, grow, and transform. Use clear drinking glasses rather than opaque pots, and opt for large seeds such as beans, beets, or peas, so you can observe every step in the process.

resealable plastic bag

paper
towels

clear
glasses

seeds

italian
bush bean

BLACK EYE PEAS

'DETROIT DARK RED'
beet

tip

You can choose
just one or both of
the methods below
to plant the seeds,
depending on
whether you have
soil. Either way,
once the seeds have
sprouted, you can
transfer them to
a pot with drainage
or plant them
outside.

SUPPLIES:

· Clear glasses
· Potting soil
· Seeds (we used
  beans, beets, and
  peas)
· Paper towels
· Reusable plastic
  bag (optional)

STEPS:

1. To plant in soil: FILL glass with damp potting soil, and
   INSERT 2 seeds close to the sides, pushing them to a depth
   of 3 times their diameter.

2. To plant between glasses: USE damp paper towels to pin
   2 seeds in place against a glass's side; INSERT a smaller glass
   to hold paper towel and seeds in place. (Seeds in damp paper
   towels will also germinate in sealed plastic bags.)

3. PLACE in a dark spot to mimic conditions underground
   until you see some growth. Then PLACE in a spot that
   receives bright natural light. KEEP soil or paper towels damp.

MOVIE MAGIC

Film buffs, take note: You don't need fancy cameras to make movies. Imagination and a bit of science will do the trick. Each of the toys on these pages uses a simple scientific notion to animate still images, making them appear to move. Give it a go and you'll be a movie producer in no time.

THAUMATROPE HOW-TO

did you know?

Many words for basic moviemaking devices come from the ancient Greek. **Thaumatrope** means "wonder turner," and it's probably the most basic of paper movies. It simply creates the illusion of two images merged into one when you spin the handle. Wonder turners are fun and fast to make: On a rainy day, you can create a bunch of new "movies" for each of your friends! Each one features a series of images that appear to come together when the stick is twirled.

SUPPLIES:

- Thaumatrope clip art (see page 336)
- White card stock
- Scissors
- Masking tape
- 16-inch-long wooden dowel (for handle)
- White craft glue

STEPS:

1. Color PHOTOCOPY the bird and cage, or the fish and bowl, clip art onto white card stock, enlarging them as instructed; CUT out disks. If you'd rather make your own, CREATE a simple pair of related images on 2 card-stock disks, making sure they line up when held back to back.

2. TAPE the dowel to the back of 1 disk so that it runs right down the center of the image. Then GLUE the second disk to the back of the first, sandwiching the dowel and aligning the images. SPIN the dowel between your palms, and watch the images merge.

did you know?

If you look at a moving **phenakistoscope,** or spindle viewer, straight on, the images will be a blur. Gaze through the slots at its reflection in a mirror, however, and your brain makes sense of the scene—and sets the designs in motion.

PHENAKISTOSCOPE HOW-TO

SUPPLIES:

- Phenakistoscope clip art (see page 337)
- Pencil, for tracing
- Heavy white paper
- Stickers, in various colors and patterns
- Markers, in various colors
- White craft glue
- Black card stock
- Scissors
- Thumbtack
- Pencil with eraser (for using as axis)

STEPS:

1. Color PHOTOCOPY the clip art onto heavy white paper, enlarging it as instructed. To make your own pattern, TRACE the clip art onto white paper, and USE stickers and markers to create a sequence of 12 images in which the starting image is also the end (we used stickers to make a clown who is losing his hat, as shown above left); each image should fit within a pie-piece shape.

2. GLUE the patterned disk onto black card stock, and CUT out disk, including the 12 slots.

3. PUSH the tack through the center of the disk and into the side of the pencil eraser, so the disk is free to SPIN. HOLD it in front of a mirror and WATCH it spin through the slots.

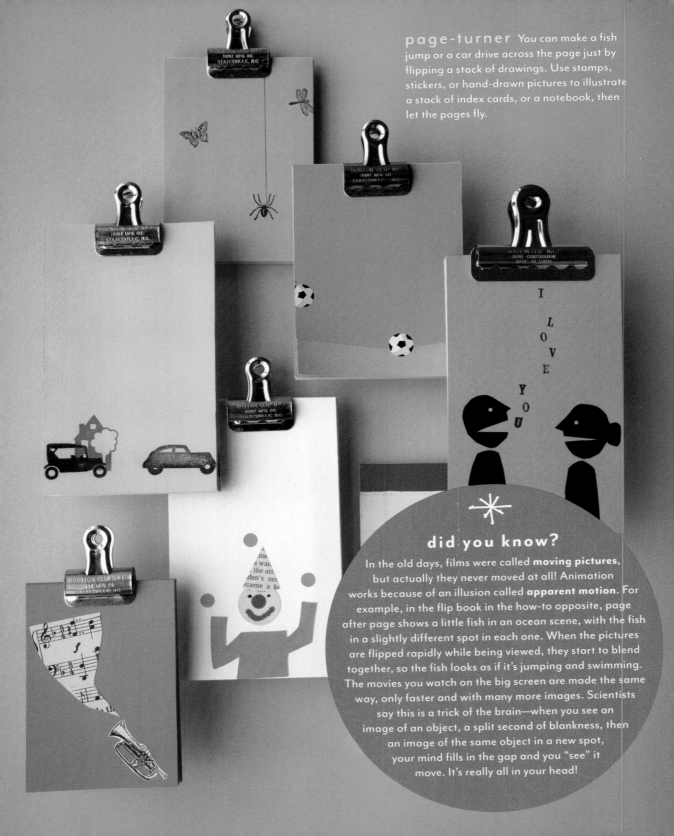

page-turner You can make a fish jump or a car drive across the page just by flipping a stack of drawings. Use stamps, stickers, or hand-drawn pictures to illustrate a stack of index cards, or a notebook, then let the pages fly.

did you know?

In the old days, films were called **moving pictures**, but actually they never moved at all! Animation works because of an illusion called **apparent motion**. For example, in the flip book in the how-to opposite, page after page shows a little fish in an ocean scene, with the fish in a slightly different spot in each one. When the pictures are flipped rapidly while being viewed, they start to blend together, so the fish looks as if it's jumping and swimming. The movies you watch on the big screen are made the same way, only faster and with many more images. Scientists say this is a trick of the brain—when you see an image of an object, a split second of blankness, then an image of the same object in a new spot, your mind fills in the gap and you "see" it move. It's really all in your head!

FLIP BOOK HOW-TO

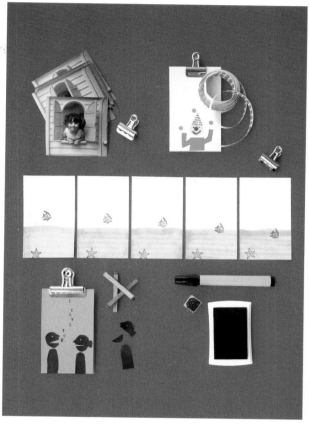

SUPPLIES:

· Index cards or notebooks

· Rubber stamps, stickers, paper cutouts, or photos

· Colored pencils or markers

· Scissors

· Bulldog clip

STEPS:

1. DECIDE what scene you want to animate, and PLAN it out.

2. CREATE your sequence of images on index cards or the pages of a notebook. You can stamp or draw, use cutouts, or trim a series of photos for your images. The images should change slightly on each card—move an element in your design (like the fish jumping, above) ⅛ inch to ⅜ inch. If it looks too jumpy when you flip the cards, MAKE additional cards whose images show smaller changes, and INSERT them in between the pages.

3. STACK the index cards for viewing, with the last page on top. SECURE with a bulldog clip. To view, FLIP from back to front.

tip

Pages from the disassembled flip book in the center (above left) show how to break motion down into steps. The sunfish starts at the top of its leap. Then it's a little farther and a little lower. It enters the water at an angle and continues to dive. Stamps, markers, stickers, and even a series of photos taken in close succession make other great flip-book images.

KEEP IT TOGETHER

Give all your collections—the everyday and the extraordinary—a home of their own, and you'll never have to go in search of them again.

ACCORDION BOXES

Small cardboard jewelry boxes are a natural choice for containing whatever tiny treasures you like to gather—stamps, buttons, stickers, and such. As long as the objects can be glued to folded pages, you're in business (see page 242 for the end result).

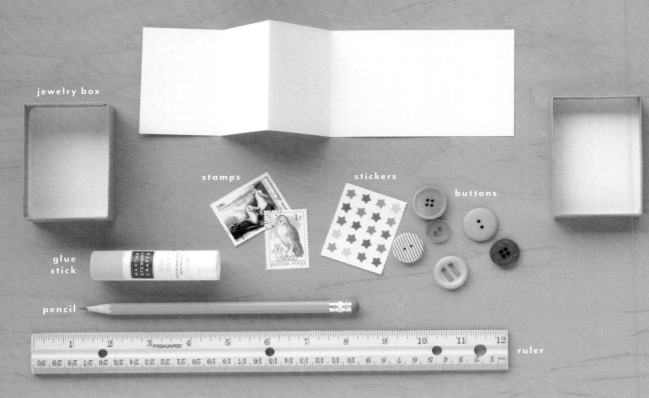

jewelry box

stamps

stickers

buttons

glue stick

pencil

ruler

heavy paper

to make the boxes

Accordion-fold a strip of heavy paper to just under the dimensions of a jewelry box, and glue the first and last pages to the inside of the box's lid and bottom. Glue small objects as desired, keeping some pages empty so the collection can grow.

MINIATURE SCRAPBOOKS

Your favorite birthday party, a great classmate, an awesome vacation—these are just some of the things you want to remember and document. Cramming every special or important moment into a scrapbook is a big job—and messy. Make things easier by creating little albums from heavyweight paper that go inside a bigger scrapbook.

to make the scrapbooks

Contrasting paper spines and corners give the albums a fancy hardcover feel. Add a closure made with a paper fastener and string, and then paste the finished albums into a full-size scrapbook.

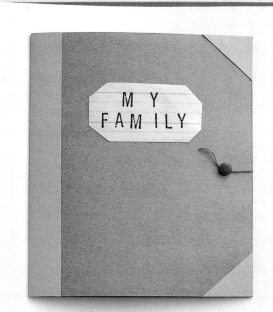

TRAVEL KEEPSAKES

Every explorer needs a place to record his or her finds. A lidded box lined with a map of the area visited will keep everything together. Tuck the box away in a special place, and you can look back whenever you want to revisit your adventure.

specimen box

Trace your trail along a map with a highlighter pen, then cut out a section of the map to fit the box's bottom. Glue in place. Use labels and tags to identify each item by location and date found. Decorate the inner and outer lid, and be sure to label the box's exterior, so it can be easily spotted on a shelf.

ring-bound books

Rather than waiting until you get home, put together little scrapbooks while you travel using a hole punch and loose-leaf rings. You might, for example, draw interesting-looking cars and trucks on plain tabs (these have prepunched holes), or record highlights on postcards. Or try tucking souvenirs into envelopes (one for each stop on a multi-stop trip), using a map cut to size for the cover; mark each city on the map with a sticker, and add a matching sticker to color-code each envelope. Punch holes in the corners of your assembled books, and hold them all together with a ring.

TRAVEL TINS

Making a vacation "scrapbox" of your seaside finds lets you take a little bit of the beach home with you. The inside of empty sardine cans are especially appropriate here; not only do they make great frames, but their labels feature classic nautical images—fish, lighthouses, and the like—that you can cut out and use to enhance the overall effect.

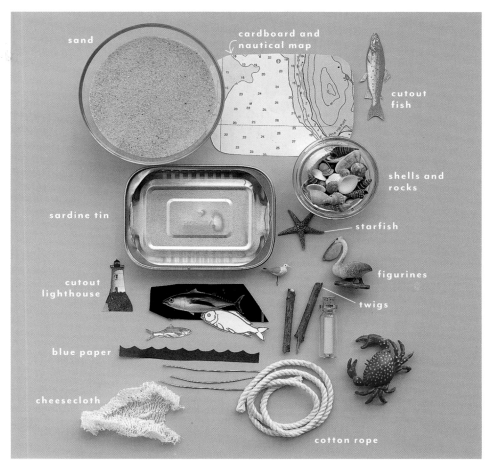

sand

cardboard and nautical map

cutout fish

sardine tin

shells and rocks

starfish

cutout lighthouse

figurines

twigs

blue paper

cheesecloth

cotton rope

SUPPLIES:

- Pencil, for tracing
- Empty cans (cleaned and dried)
- Cardboard
- Nautical map
- Scissors
- White craft glue
- Shells, twigs, rocks, toy birds and shellfish, other nautical figurines, cheesecloth, and cutout images
- Card stock
- Sand
- Blue construction paper
- Thin rope
- Duct tape

STEPS:

1. For background, TRACE bottom of sardine can onto cardboard and onto a nautical map, and CUT out; GLUE map onto cardboard, then GLUE inside can.

2. GLUE on shells, figurines, cutout images, and cheesecloth (to resemble a net). To make free-floating fish, GLUE fish cutout to one end of card stock strip folded at each end; GLUE other end to background.

3. BRUSH glue on floor of diorama; SPRINKLE with sand or add waves cut from blue construction paper (make tabs on bottom for attaching to tin). GLUE rope or shells to border of cans or leave plain. To hang diorama, TAPE rope to back.

TREASURE CHEST

Aaargh! Don't let your best beachy souvenirs wash out to sea; stash them away pirate style. Use canceled stamps—available from hobby shops and online—to make a nautical scene on the inside of a box lid. Then fill the box with your booty.

SUPPLIES:

- Cardboard box with hinged top
- Paint or markers
- Canceled postage stamps
- Sand

STEPS:

1. CREATE a seaside scene on the inside of the lid of the box with paint or markers and stamps. We arranged stamps to make two clipper ships and a sun.

2. ADD sand to the bottom of the box. NESTLE your treasures in the sand.

MEMORY JARS

Keep vacation memories a little stronger a lot longer by filling clear glass jars with items picked up on vacations, using one for each trip (and labeling with the date and destination, if desired). Wide-mouth jars make it easy to arrange the items inside; bent wire can be used to lower and position objects in a jar with a narrow neck.

SCHOOL-WORK SCRAPBOOKS

What better way to document a child's progress through school than with a series of albums filled with the most notable accomplishments and other memories? Use binders with clear sleeves and a clear cover; label each with a different grade and the school photo from that year. Fill with significant papers or written projects, report cards, and awards.

CEREAL BOX ORGANIZERS

Kids go through boxes of cereal fast. Make use of all the empty boxes by turning them into handy desktop organizers. Large boxes work well for books, small ones for supplies.

SUPPLIES:

- Empty cereal boxes in various sizes
- Utility knife
- Wrapping paper or contact paper
- Scissors
- Double-sided tape

STEPS:

1. Have an adult CUT box with a utility knife at desired angle and height. USE large boxes for holding notebooks and folders, cutting them on a diagonal at top. USE smaller boxes for pencils, rulers, and such. For index cards, LAY a small box on its side and CUT off the top.

2. WRAP decorative paper around box to see how much you'll need; UNWRAP and CUT to fit. SECURE paper with double-sided tape; TRIM excess.

TACK-FREE BULLETIN BOARD

This board has colorful appeal: Crisscrossed rubber bands let you arrange your latest snapshots, notes from friends, and artwork. Plus, you don't have to make holes in these significant papers, since no thumbtacks are used to hold them in place.

SUPPLIES:

· Acrylic paint and paintbrush
· 1-foot square of corkboard
· Extra-long colored rubber bands

STEPS:

1. PAINT both sides of corkboard and LET dry completely.

2. STRETCH extra-long rubber bands lengthwise and widthwise over the corkboard, making sure the rubber bands go over and under one another at intervals.

3. TUCK photos, artwork, notes, and more under the bands.

POCKET BOOKS

Are you a list-maker? A journal writer? Some kids are inclined to bursts of creative genius and need places to jot it all down. Why not store all that inspiration in one fun place? Mini books—with covers made from postcards, wrapping paper, maps, magazine pages, or printouts of favorite photos—can speak volumes about your favorite things and are nice to look at, too. Fold them over white paper so there's a place to write, then staple in the center. Slip the books inside clear plastic pocketed sheets, made for baseball cards or photos, and store in a three-ring binder.

TINY TRINKET BOXES

Even the most minuscule collectibles deserve a dedicated box—to keep them safe and show off their infinite charms. Sliding cardboard matchboxes—covered with scanned images of the contents, for easy identification—are perfect for the job.

a good cover To give your label an interesting background, lay a piece of paper over the objects on the scanner. Use a bright or dark paper with light-colored items so they'll stand out.

SUPPLIES:

- Empty matchboxes, in a variety of sizes
- Scanner
- Colored paper or peel-and-stick paper
- Scissors
- Glue stick

STEPS:

1. CHOOSE an empty matchbox that will hold the items you need to store.

2. SELECT items for the label, and place on the scanner. TRY a few arrangements: You might LAY the objects down randomly or line them up to make a border. Then SCAN the image into the computer.

3. PRINT the image onto colored paper, or onto peel-and-stick paper (it comes in many colors, as well as clear).

4. TRIM the printout to fit around the container. If using regular paper, apply glue to the back of the label. STICK the label on the container, starting at one end and smoothing it out with your hand. TRIM excess. ADD your treasures to the tiny box.

PORTABLE CUBBY

It's easier to focus on the task at hand, especially in a busy room, when you have a fold-up homework center like this one. Add folders and clips to keep essentials in place.

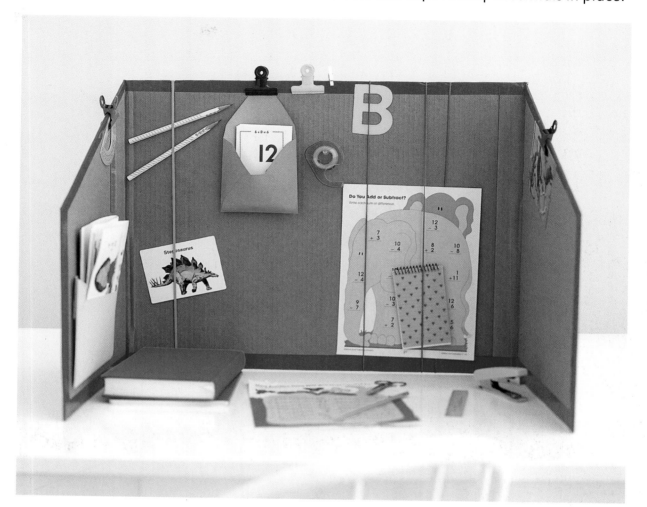

SUPPLIES:

- Large cardboard box
- Utility knife
- Colored duct tape
- Extra-long rubber bands
- Binder clips
- Thumbtacks

STEPS:

1. An adult should CUT up the large box with a utility knife, removing the bottom, top, and one long side.

2. TRIM the height, then slope the sides of the cubby.

3. FINISH edges with colored duct tape. ATTACH rubber bands to run the height of the cubby, and clips and tacks to help organize notes, calendars, and other items.

COIN COUNTERS

Baby-food jars are just the right size for mini coin banks. Using one for each type of coin is a fun way to sort your collection. Have a grown-up use a utility knife to cut a slit in each lid large enough for coins to slide through; press the rough slits flat against underside of lid using needle-nose pliers. In a well-ventilated area, spray-paint lids with latex paint; when dry, use a marker and a stencil to indicate 1, 5, 10, and 25 cents.

BOTTLE PIGGY BANKS

Pigs are known for gobbling things up. Rather than leaving loose change lying around, you can make this pair of hungry piggy banks—one for spending money, one for savings—using wide-mouth plastic bottles. It's a great way to recycle, as well.

SUPPLIES:

- Scissors
- Colored and patterned paper
- Water bottles
- White craft glue
- Bottle Piggy Banks templates (see page 340)
- Utility knife
- Hole punch
- Wooden beads

STEPS:

1. CUT a piece of paper into a long, wide strip. WRAP it around the bottle; GLUE in place. An adult should use a utility knife to CUT a slot in the top for coins.

2. Use templates to CUT out inner and outer ear shapes from paper; GLUE together. BEND back bottom of ear; GLUE to bottle.

3. Use a hole punch to CUT eyes from black paper and nostrils from pink; GLUE in place.

4. To make feet, GLUE beads to the paper on the bottom of the bank; let dry.

LEAF ALPHABET

As easy as A,B,C: Gather leaves in a variety of shapes, colors, and sizes, arrange them into creatures and other shapes, then glue them to card-stock alphabet cards. This makes an excellent display-worthy project for a classroom full of kids.

Bb

butterflies

Cc

Christmas

Dd

deer

Ee

elephant

Ff

fish

Gg

grasshopper

Hh

hair

Ii

insect

Jj

juggler

Kk

kite

Ll

love

Mm

moustache

Nn

necklace

Oo

oranges

Pp

peacock

Qq

quail

Rr rooster

Ss sparrow

Tt tree

Uu umbrella

Vv violin

Ww whale

Xx xylophone

Yy yacht

Zz Zack

clever reuse
Running out of wall space? You can also laminate the leaf collages with clear adhesive paper, and use them as place mats, as shown at left, or make them into a book.

LEAF ALPHABET HOW-TO

SUPPLIES:

- Leaves in a variety of colors, shapes, and sizes
- Heavy books
- Telephone book or newspaper
- Heavy paper or card stock
- Scissors
- Glue stick or white craft glue
- Pencil and pen

STEPS:

1. COLLECT leaves, avoiding ones with any mold or rot. LAY leaves flat between pages of a phone book or layers of newspaper, then WEIGHT them with heavy books. ALLOW 1 to 2 weeks to fully flatten and dry. If you live in an area without many leaves (or want to enhance your collection), you can BUY leaves online, already pressed, from floral suppliers.

2. ARRANGE leaves on a piece of heavy paper in shapes according to the alphabet. EXPERIMENT with combinations of colors and shapes. EMBELLISH designs by cutting notches for parts like mouths, tails, and fins; CUT out those details from spare leaves.

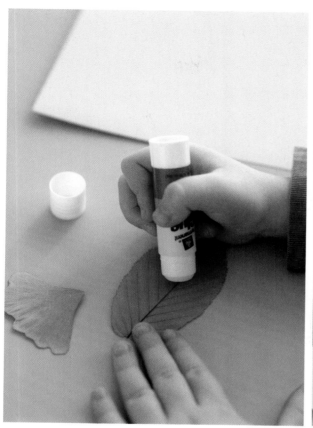

3. GLUE leaves into place with glue stick or white glue. LAY a clean sheet of paper on top of glued leaves and RUB gently to SMOOTH and FLATTEN. Carefully REMOVE the top sheet.

4. LABEL the artwork: An adult can use a pencil to SKETCH in guidelines for the letters and the word; a kid can then WRITE the words in ink. KEEP the artwork flat when it is complete, because pressed leaves can be brittle. DISPLAY alphabet collages on a bulletin board or wall.

CHAPTER 7

GIVE SOMETHING HANDMADE

Whether it's a personalized bag, a box of fudge, or a cross-stitched family portrait, the best gifts are always the ones you make yourself.

CROSS-STITCH FAMILY PORTRAITS

These handmade portraits will have your family and friends in stitches (literally). Cross-stitching is easier and faster than it looks—if you can sew on a button, you can do it. Use graph paper to plan your people from head to toe. Then thread your needle and start X-ing your loved ones off your list.

CROSS-STITCH HOW-TO

tips for cross-stiching

- The special cloth you use for cross-stitch is called Aida cloth. If you're new to cross-stitch, get a lower-count Aida cloth, such as 8 (which has 8 squares per linear inch). It allows for bigger stitches and makes for larger figures. A higher count, such as 14, requires smaller stitches.

- Embroidery floss is several smaller strands twisted together that can be separated: Thread your needle with 4 of these strands for 8-count cloth, and 2 for 14-count (for backstitching, use 2 strands for 8-count, 1 for 14-count).

- Always begin by plotting out your design on graph paper: One square represents one cross-stitch. Use our examples on pages 338 and 339 as a guide, and then improvise.

- We found that it works well to make adults' heads 10 stitches across and kids' heads 9 stitches across. Babies' are even smaller— just 3 stitches across. Eye spacing and mouth size can vary with age, too.

- In cross-stitch, as in life, hairdos tend to capture the essence of a person. Play around until you perfect your sister's pigtails or your grandpa's bushy beard.

- French knots make great buttons and baby eyes (see page 145 for the how-to).

- Backstitching (see Basic Sewing Techniques, pages 144–145) lets you add small details, such as eyeglass frames, shirt collars, kite and balloon strings, and labels.

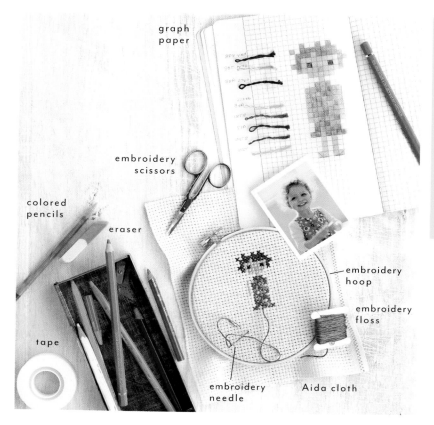

graph paper

embroidery scissors

colored pencils

eraser

tape

embroidery needle

embroidery hoop

embroidery floss

Aida cloth

SUPPLIES:

- Cross-stitch Family Portraits templates (see pages 338–339)
- Color photo(s)
- Graph paper
- Colored pencils and eraser
- Clear tape
- Embroidery floss in a variety of colors
- Aida cloth
- 4-inch embroidery hoop
- Embroidery needle
- Embroidery scissors

STEPS:

1. Following our templates, or using your own pattern, PLOT out your design on graph paper (as instructed, opposite). CHOOSE your colors and embroidery floss. CENTER cloth in an embroidery hoop. COUNT the stitches in each row of your pattern.

2. Using the fabric's weave as a grid, SEW that number of stitches: First CREATE a row of evenly spaced diagonal lines, then STITCH back over the row, creating Xs. To make a three-quarter cross-stitch (for an open shirt collar, say), MAKE the first stitch from the corner to the square's middle, and then the second stitch as normal.

3. Continue stitching according to your pattern. When the design is complete, TRIM excess cloth. DISPLAY in embroidery hoop, or remove and frame.

IRON-ON TRANSFER TOTES

Adorned with a drawing, plain cotton bags—like the ones you carry to the grocery store, the beach, and the soccer field—make great gifts for friends and family members. Smaller bags and cloth cases can also be embellished.

to make the bags

You can decorate a bag with just one great picture, or pick a single drawing and duplicate it several times. To start, scan the artwork or draw an image using your computer's art program. Resize as needed, then print the image onto iron-on transfer paper (available at office-supply stores) made to fit an ink-jet printer. Trim the design, and then an adult should use a dry iron to transfer the image to a clean canvas bag (follow the manufacturer's instructions for transferring and setting).

MONOGRAMMED TOTE

Teachers' gifts, while greatly appreciated, often tend to look alike. But this practical, one-of-a-kind present is sure to be remembered—and put to good use. Add an initial in a pretty fabric that's ironed on (no sewing required).

to make a tote

Print an initial from a computer, enlarge it further on a photocopier as necessary, and then cut it out to make a pattern. Back fabric with fusible webbing, following the package directions. Lay the initial facedown on the webbing side of the fabric; trace, and cut out. Center the letter on a tote bag, and have an adult iron on. Finish with a ribbon and a tag with your handwritten greeting.

ARTFUL ACCESSORIES

Brighten your favorite grown-up's day by giving his or her desk essentials a creative makeover, using your most cheerful drawings. Choose a colorful picture from the refrigerator door, or draw a new one specifically for the occasion.

to make a pencil cup

For an eye-catching catchall, clean and dry a can from the recycling bin and peel off the label. Scan or color photocopy artwork, resizing as needed. Wrap around can (it should overlap itself a bit). Seal with glue stick or tape.

to make checkbook and passport covers

Start with clear passport or checkbook sleeves, available from stationery stores and online retailers. Scan or color photocopy artwork, resizing as needed. Using a cover as a template, trace outline over a section of the image. Cut out, following just inside the traced line, then slip the picture into the cover.

CANDY WRAPPERS

You don't always have to start from scratch when it comes to handcrafting gifts—especially gifts in multiples. For Valentine's Day, begin with store-bought candy but express yourself with pretty papers, stickers, ribbons, and other easy embellishments.

to make the wrappers

Tuck gum inside a card-stock "matchbook"—cut card stock into a rectangle, fold up bottom 1 inch and staple, then fold paper in half—stamped with a message. (Sticks of gum sold in large packs often have plain white wrappers that are perfect for decorating.)

Adorn a lollipop with a sticker and tape it to a card-stock heart; slip a sheet of button candy into a small paper bag embellished with die-cut scrap art (available at crafts stores) or a sticker.

Wrap a candy bar in a band of patterned paper and tie with twine. Don't forget to include a note—on the underside or on a tag attached with waxed twine.

I CHEW-SE YOU !

LOVE YOU
LOVE YOU

FOLDED HEARTS

For a heart-shaped take on the tried-and-true love note, make the envelope itself the valentine.

SUPPLIES:

- Scissors
- Patterned paper (with one side plain)
- Crayon, marker, or colored pencil
- Stickers

STEPS:

1. CUT a wide heart shape from the paper—wrapping paper works well. WRITE a message on the plain side. ADD heart stickers or DRAW your own hearts. FOLD in both sides as shown.

2. FOLD the top down just above the middle, and then TURN the envelope so the point is at the top.

3. FOLD the point down. SEAL with a sticker.

CUSTOM CANDY BAGS

With just a few supplies and a couple bags of bulk candy, you can put together treat packages emblazoned with your own image—puckering up, no less!—in no time.

you're sweet !
xo
sammy

to make the candy bags

Resize and print a picture onto heavyweight matte paper. Cut into rectangular strips for tags, using pinking shears for the short ends; draw hearts, and stamp a message on the back of each one. Fold the tags and tape them to cellophane bags filled with sweets.

BUTTON BOBBY PINS

For girls who love to accessorize (and who doesn't?), pretty hair clips are sure to be in demand, so you may as well make a whole bunch all at once.

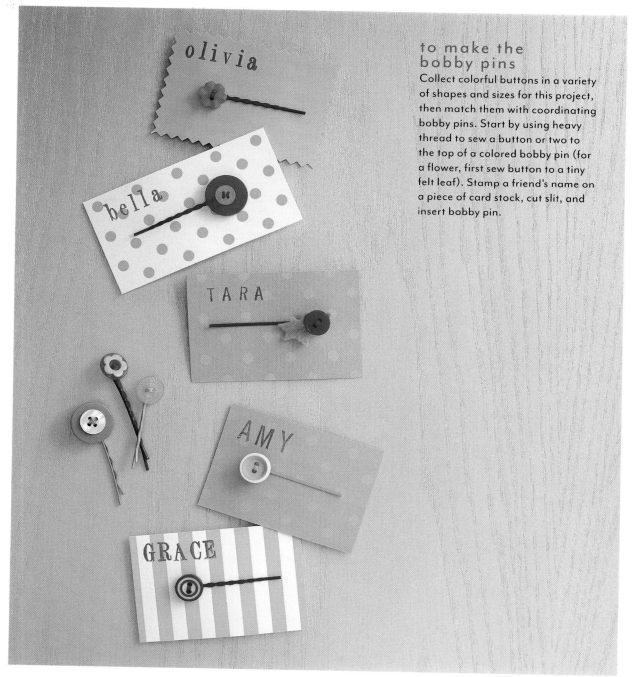

to make the bobby pins

Collect colorful buttons in a variety of shapes and sizes for this project, then match them with coordinating bobby pins. Start by using heavy thread to sew a button or two to the top of a colored bobby pin (for a flower, first sew button to a tiny felt leaf). Stamp a friend's name on a piece of card stock, cut slit, and insert bobby pin.

CREPE-PAPER BUNNIES

Need party favors for a spring fling? Hop to it! These round little rabbits are made of tightly wound crepe-paper strips; as guests unwind them, they'll find surprises—such as tiny toys and candies—hidden inside.

HOW-TO

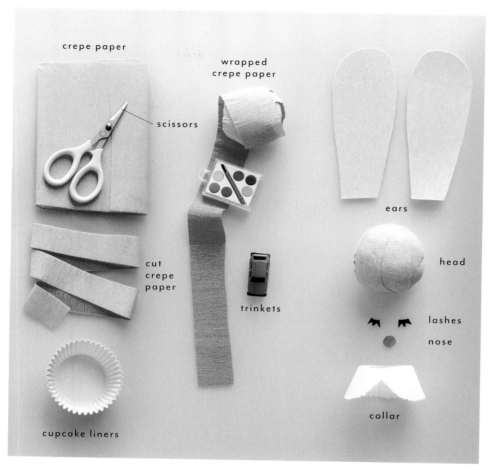

crepe paper

wrapped crepe paper

scissors

cut crepe paper

trinkets

cupcake liners

ears

head

lashes

nose

collar

SUPPLIES:

- **Crepe-Paper Bunnies templates** (see page 340)
- **Scissors**
- **Crepe paper** (sold in sheets called *folds*)
- **Trinkets**
- **Low-temperature glue gun**
- **Clear glue**
- **Tissue or construction paper**
- **Paper cupcake liners**

STEPS:

1. Using template, CUT 2 bunny ears from crepe paper. CUT the rest of the sheet crosswise into ¾-inch-wide strips.

2. WRAP one strip around a trinket, creating a ball. (Ask an adult to hot-glue ends of paper together as needed.) ADD another trinket every few layers. CONTINUE until head is the size of a tennis ball. Secure end of strip with clear glue.

3. PINCH bottoms of ears and GLUE to ball with glue gun. Use templates to CUT lashes and nose from tissue paper, and GLUE in place.

4. SNIP away center of cupcake liner so head rests inside. CUT fluted part to create collar. GLUE in place.

BABY-CHICK BEANBAGS

Cheep cheep! Little beanbag hatchlings—popping out of plastic eggs—are so cute that you might feel bad about tossing them around after the egg hunt. But they're also too much fun to resist. Yellow split peas have the best texture for filling. If you're using cotton fabric, add a liner so the peas don't show through; with felt, this isn't necessary.

fabric

yellow split peas

disappearing-ink fabric pen

funnel

beak

wings

screw punch

fabric glue

SUPPLIES:

- Scissors
- Baby-Chick Beanbags templates (see page 340)
- Felt for body and accents (or colored cotton fabric, plus white cotton for liner)
- Disappearing-ink fabric pen
- Needle and thread
- Small funnel
- Yellow split peas
- Pinking shears
- Iron
- Screw punch
- Fabric glue

STEPS:

1. CUT fabric rectangles slightly larger than the body template; you'll need 2 felt pieces, or 2 colored cotton and 2 white cotton pieces. STACK the pieces; if using cotton, STACK them as you want them to appear on the finished chick, with colored fabric on top and bottom. USE disappearing-ink pen to trace the template onto the top piece. HANDSTITCH ¼ inch inside the line, leaving a small opening at one end.

2. USE a funnel to fill the shape with split peas. STITCH the opening closed. TRIM along the line using pinking shears.

3. For the beak, FOLD a small piece of felt in half; an adult should iron to crease. PLACE beak template on the fold, and CUT out. USE wing template to cut 2 wings. USE screw punch to make 2 eyes from dark felt. GLUE on pieces.

SCENTED SCRUB

Give the gift of indulgence. It's one-size-fits-all and guaranteed to bring pure bliss to your mom or anyone else who deserves a bit of pampering.

spoon

glass jar

tip ✳

To scent homemade beauty items, you'll need essential oils, available at health-food shops and from online retailers. Use scents alone or in combinations; if mixing scents, add the oil with the less-intense scent first, followed by the stronger kind, one drop at a time. Here are a few of our favorites: citrus (grapefruit, lemon, or tangerine); geranium; lavender; eucalyptus; peppermint; rosemary; and star anise.

essential oils

Epsom and coarse sea salts

SUPPLIES:

- Large bowl
- Coarse sea salt
- Epsom salts
- Baking soda
- Spoon
- Essential oil(s)
- Lidded glass jar
- Label
- Colored twine or ribbon

STEPS:

1. In a large bowl, MIX to combine: 6 parts coarse sea salt, 3 parts Epsom salts, and 1 part baking soda.

2. ADD a few drops of essential oils (use very sparingly; see above), and stir to combine.

3. Divide salts among lidded glass jars. Label each with a handwritten tag, and TIE with twine or ribbon.

LIP BALM

These pretty little tins of homemade lip balm are all-natural, custom-scented and -colored, and easy to produce. To dress up plain metal pots or slide tins, just stick on some colorful adhesive dots in a variety of sizes and colors.

tip

Chances are, you already have one or more carrier oils—so called because they help distribute the essential oil and create a smooth texture—in your kitchen: grapeseed oil (virtually odorless), sunflower oil, olive oil (choose the lightest grades so the scent won't mask that of the essential oil), and vitamin E oil (which can be expensive, so use in small quantities in combination with another carrier oil).

carrier oil

essential oil

lipstick

eyeliner

beeswax pellets

pipette

SUPPLIES:

- 1 tablespoon beeswax pellets (available at crafts stores)
- 2 tablespoons carrier oil (see Tip, opposite)
- Heatproof glass jar
- Pot
- Metal spoon
- Plastic pipettes
- Essential oil(s)
- Store-bought lipstick and eyeliner (for color)
- Craft stick (for shaving lipstick)
- Cosmetic-style slide tins or metal pots (available from online packaging suppliers)

STEPS:

1. PUT 1 tablespoon beeswax and 2 tablespoons carrier oil in jar, and CLOSE lid. An adult should HEAT the jar in a pot of water over medium-low until wax has melted. REMOVE jar from pot carefully.

2. STIR mixture with a metal spoon. Using a pipette, ADD essential oil, 1 drop at a time, until strength of scent is to your liking. SHAVE off small amounts of lipstick and liner with a craft stick, then STIR in shavings, one at a time, until desired shade is achieved.

3. Using another pipette, TRANSFER lip balm to cosmetic containers. Let set for 1 hour.

4. Once balm in container has set, you can MAKE patterns with melted balm in another color: For dots, USE a straw to poke holes in balm; REMOVE excess wax from tin with a toothpick, then USE a pipette to fill hole with melted balm; let set. For stripes, CUT away balm with a knife and PIPE in a different color.

tips

This makes enough to fill two .15-ounce tubes and two .5-ounce tins or pots. To make more than one kind of lip balm at a time, or to make patterns as shown opposite, divide the recipe in half and scent and color the batches separately. For lip balms, use essential oils that have an "edible" scent, such as citrus.

BUTTON FRAMES

Put a collection of favorite buttons to good use: Glue them onto a basic white picture frame and then tuck a drawing or photo inside for grandparents to proudly display. Choose buttons in assorted sizes and colors for an eye-catching arrangement, and lay them all in place before you start gluing to ensure a good fit.

CUSTOM NOTEPAD

A pad of paper for jotting down notes and reminders is an office and entryway essential. Use a big block notepad as a canvas for your creativity, and you have a useful *and* personal gift. Dad will think of you every time he puts pen to paper.

to customize a notepad

Wrap a rubber band around a notepad cube, to hold the pages together, and then write greetings and draw pictures on 2 sides using a broad-tip marker. (Fine tips will get caught between the pages.) Move rubber band, and decorate the other 2 sides. Tie the notepad with a colorful ribbon. As an added gift, slide a pen under the bow.

FRAMED STAMP ART

Snail-mail might seem like ancient history, but stamps are still cool—and fun to collect. Rather than storing them away in albums, use a few to create some framable wall art.

tip
Buy inexpensive packages of canceled stamps from hobby shops and online dealers, or collect envelopes that have come in the mail. (To remove stamp, cut away the envelope and soak in lukewarm water for 10 minutes, or until the stamp floats off. Blot dry with paper towels.)

SUPPLIES:

- Canceled postage stamps
- Paper towels
- Scissors
- Art paper
- Crayons or markers
- Paint
- Paintbrushes
- White craft glue or permanent glue stick
- Heavy book
- Frame

STEPS:

1. DECIDE on the design you want to create: Let the color or motifs of the stamps inspire you. ARRANGE stamps according to your design, trimming them as necessary. Complete design with crayons, markers, and paint, as desired.

2. GLUE the stamps in place, then PUT a heavy book on your artwork for an hour to help the stamps adhere and get the picture to dry flat. Frame artwork, trimming as necessary.

JULY 4TH ROCKET FAVORS

Blast off! These lively candy-filled spaceships make playful favor packages for a patriotic parade-watching party. And you don't have to be a rocket scientist to make one—they're easy to put together with colorful clip art and basic supplies.

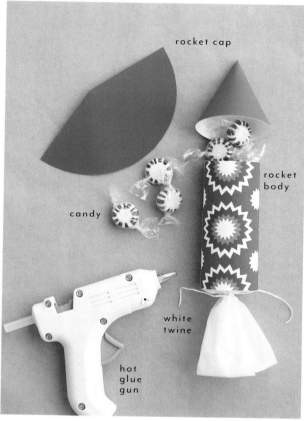

SUPPLIES:

- July 4th Rocket Favors clip art (see page 340)
- White card stock
- Scissors
- Double-sided tape
- White tissue paper
- Twine or string
- Low-temperature hot-glue gun
- Wrapped peppermint candy

STEPS:

1. PRINT the clip art onto card stock; CUT out the shapes.

2. PLACE the rectangular clip art blank side up. AFFIX tape to 1 long edge. FOLD a piece of tissue paper in half (so it measures 4 by 5½ inches). PLACE the tissue fold at the bottom of the card stock, pressing it to the tape to secure.

3. ROLL the card stock and tissue into a cylinder shape, and SECURE with tape. CINCH the tissue at the bottom of the rocket, and TIE it with twine.

4. ROLL fan-shaped clip art into a cone; SECURE with hot glue. PLACE candies inside rocket. Have an adult GLUE cone to body. Let dry completely.

HALLOWEEN FAVOR TREE

Trick? No way! Treat your friends by dangling Halloween party favors right in front of their eyes. Arrange a bucket of gnarly tree branches on a side table to display handcrafted evil-eyed black cats, jolly jack-o'-lanterns, and candy-filled sacks for each person to take.

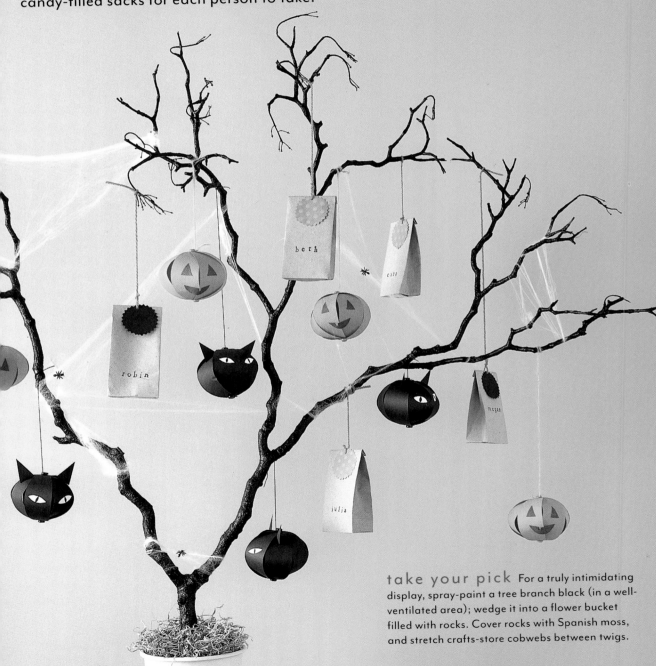

take your pick For a truly intimidating display, spray-paint a tree branch black (in a well-ventilated area); wedge it into a flower bucket filled with rocks. Cover rocks with Spanish moss, and stretch crafts-store cobwebs between twigs.

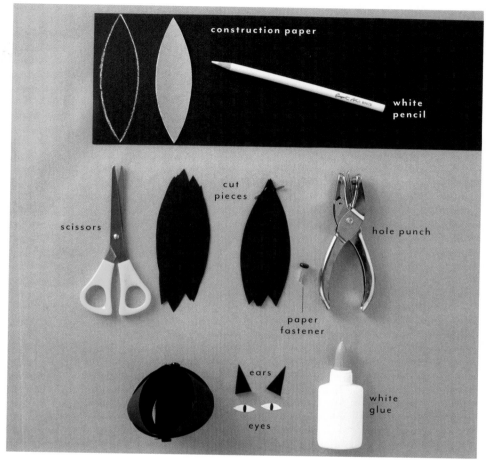

SUPPLIES:

- White pencil
- Halloween Favor Tree template (see page 341)
- Construction paper in black and orange
- Scissors
- Hole punch
- Paper fasteners in black or orange
- White craft glue
- Small alphabet stamps
- Ink pad
- Mini paper bags
- Pinking shears
- Patterned paper
- Candy
- Yarn

STEPS:

1. For each ornament, use white pencil to TRACE template onto construction paper 7 times. CUT out.

2. STACK pieces, and PUNCH holes through both ends with the punch; INSERT a black or orange paper fastener through holes.

3. BEND stack into a C shape; FAN out pieces to form a globe. GLUE on paper features (for cat's ears, fold bottom under to make a tab).

4. For favors, STAMP mini paper bags with names. Using pinking shears, CUT traced circles out of patterned paper. FILL bags with candy; FOLD over tops. PLACE a circle on each; PUNCH a hole through all layers. TIE on yarn for hanging.

PUMPKIN TAKE-AWAY TREATS

Ever made a jack-o'-lantern from an apple? The grinning pumpkin faces on these muslin treat bags were stamped from small apples (called lady apples) that were carved into faces and dipped in ink. An adult should help with the knife work.

foam
brush

triangular
makeup
sponge

lady
apple

acrylic
paint

utility
knife

muslin bag

washcloth

SUPPLIES:

· Lady apple
· Utility knife
· Paper towels
· Orange and green
  acrylic paint
· Foam brush
· Small drawstring
  muslin bags
· Washcloth
· Triangular makeup
  sponge

STEPS:

1. An adult should do this step: CUT apple vertically, just off center to avoid core and seeds. Using a utility knife, CARVE out a jack-o'-lantern face.

2. BLOT stamp dry with a paper towel, then APPLY a thin layer of orange acrylic paint with a foam brush. LAY a bag on a washcloth, and STAMP with apple.

3. To CREATE the stem shape, CUT off the tip of a makeup sponge; DIP in green paint, and STAMP. Let dry.

GHOULISH GOODIES

Kids are so busy running from house to house on Halloween night, they don't often consider what's being handed out at their own door. But dressing up the candy you're giving away makes for some wicked fun. These crafts double as finger puppets once the candy inside has disappeared.

skull   bat   ghost

SUPPLIES:

- Ghoulish Goodies templates (see page 341)
- Pencil
- Scissors
- White and black construction paper
- Mini candy bars
- Double-sided tape
- Black and red felt-tip pens
- White gel pen

STEPS:

1. Use templates to TRACE skull and bones, bat body and wings, or ghost body and arms onto white or black paper; CUT out.

2. WRAP body pieces around mini candy bars, securing with double-sided tape. TAPE bones, wings, or arms to backs of their bodies. (When making bats, FOLD wings at the midpoint of either side for dimension.)

3. DRAW facial features onto goodies, using a black felt-tip pen for skulls and ghosts and a white gel pen and red felt-tip pen for bats.

SNOWMEN CANDY BARS

Sweet! Here's a holiday gift that's on everyone's list (or should be!), and it's easy on the allowance to boot. Wrap store-bought chocolate bars in cheerful outfits, and use your fingertips to stamp on facial features. Hand out to classmates or as holiday party favors.

SUPPLIES:

· Chocolate bars
· White text-weight paper
· Clear or double-sided tape
· Black ink pads
· Orange marker
· Red yarn or rickrack
· Scissors

STEPS:

1. WRAP bar in white paper, taping seams. PRESS your fingertip in black ink, and STAMP eyes, mouth, and buttons. DRAW a triangle nose with orange marker.

2. For scarf, WRAP yarn or rickrack around bar, then KNOT and TRIM to desired length.

GUMDROP LOLLIPOPS

Sparkling gumdrop characters create a wintry wonderland to behold: Make them the centerpiece of a cheerful holiday display by arranging a few on a sanding sugar–covered flower frog in a clear glass jar. Then let visiting friends take their pick. Simply slide gumdrops onto candy sticks to create the body of each pop, and embellish away (the candy is so sticky that cut pieces will stick to one another without any glue). Just try not to eat up all your supplies as you work!

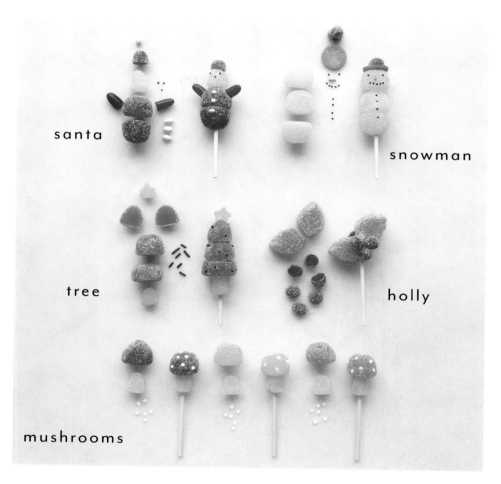

to make santa

Use top half of 1 small red gumdrop for hat and 2 larger ones for body. Trim 2 red oblong candies (such as Hot Tamales) for arms. Use candy-coated seeds for buttons and pom-pom. Poke candy with a skewer where facial features will go; use sticky tip to pick up and place nonpareils for eyes and nose.

to make a snowman

Trim top of large white gumdrop for head; top with 1 black candy wafer and half of 1 small black gumdrop for hat. Use 2 larger gumdrops for body. Using a skewer (see Santa instructions, left), place nonpareils for eyes, mouth, and buttons. Insert sprinkle for nose.

to make holly

Use green leaf-shaped gumdrops and halves of small red gumdrops for berries.

to make a tree

Use 2 flattened green gumdrops for base of tree. Use 1 small yellow gumdrop for trunk. For treetop, cut sides from 1 green gumdrop and press sides around top of stick. Flatten 1 yellow gumdrop; using an aspic cutter, cut out star. Insert red sprinkles all over for lights.

to make mushrooms

Use 1 small white gumdrop for each stem. Use sequin sprinkles for dots on red, yellow, or orange gumdrop caps.

MATCHBOX GIFTS

Tiny boxes inspire wonder: They're easy to hide, and they can hold all sorts of toys, trinkets, and treats (don't forget to include a note in each box). And kids can wrap them all by themselves, with almost no help from their grown-ups.

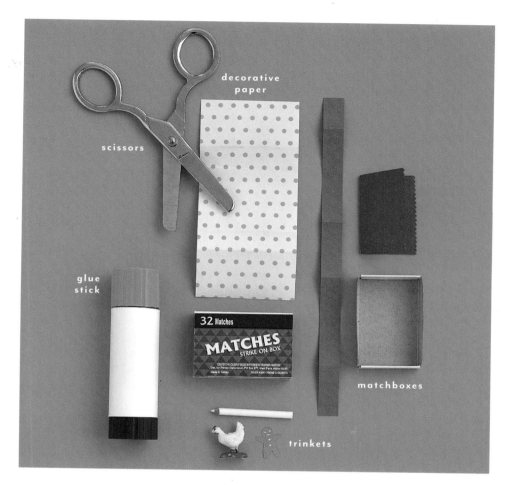

SUPPLIES:

- Matchboxes (available in bulk at grocery or discount stores), emptied
- Scissors
- Decorative paper
- Glue stick
- Colored string or twine
- Pinking shears
- Trinkets

STEPS:

1. For a standard-size matchbox, CUT a 3¾-by-2-inch band of decorative paper.

2. GLUE band around box; you can also attach a strip of paper around inner box. EMBELLISH with string, stickers, or a thin strip of paper glued around box.

3. MAKE a card to go inside: CUT a 2-by-2½-inch piece of paper; TRIM edges with pinking shears, if desired, and FOLD in half. Fill box with a trinket or two.

CHOCOLATE FUDGE

Delight teachers, neighbors, classmates, and everyone else on your gift list with a box of homemade chocolate fudge. We cut ours into snowflakes, but you can use small cutters to make other shapes as well, or simply cut into squares. Pack a few pieces into a box lined with waxed paper (to avoid sticking), and tie it with a color-coordinated ribbon.

to make the fudge

INGREDIENTS:

- 2 cups granulated sugar
- 1 teaspoon salt
- 6 tablespoons unsalted butter
- 1 cup heavy cream
- 3½ cups mini marshmallows
- 3 cups semisweet chocolate chips
- 1 teaspoon pure vanilla extract
- Confectioners' sugar, for dusting
- Vegetable oil cooking spray

DIRECTIONS:

1. Coat a 9-by-13-inch baking pan with cooking spray. Line with parchment paper, leaving overhang on each long side; coat evenly with cooking spray. Combine granulated sugar, salt, butter, cream, and marshmallows in a heavy-bottomed medium saucepan. Cook over medium heat, stirring with a wooden spoon, until butter and marshmallows are almost melted, and mixture starts to boil, 5 to 6 minutes. Continue to boil, stirring occasionally, 5 minutes more. An adult should remove the pan from the heat.

2. Add chocolate chips and vanilla to saucepan. Stir until chips are melted and combined. An adult should pour hot fudge into the prepared pan. Cool fudge in the pan, at room temperature, at least 3 hours (or up to overnight, covered with plastic wrap). MAKES ENOUGH FOR ABOUT 16 TWO-INCH PIECES

SUPPLIES:

- Fudge recipe and ingredients (right)
- Cutting board
- 2-inch snowflake cookie cutter
- Fine-mesh sieve
- Confectioners' sugar
- Boxes, ribbons, and waxed paper (for packaging)

STEPS:

1. REMOVE fudge from pan, using parchment to lift it, and PLACE on a cutting board.

2. USE a cookie cutter to CUT out snowflake shapes from fudge, cutting them as close together as possible.

3. With the sieve, DUST tops of snowflakes with confectioners' sugar. (Fudge will keep at room temperature up to 10 days in an airtight container.)

HAND-EMBELLISHED
HANDKERCHIEFS

Season's greetings last a whole lot longer
when they are drawn onto hankies.
Folded and tied, they double as holiday
cards of the most heartfelt kind.

HOW-TO

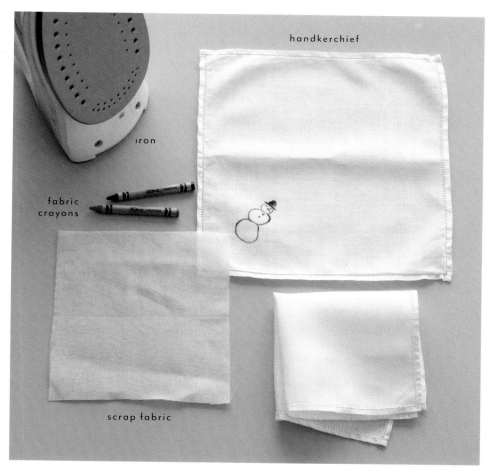

handkerchief

iron

fabric
crayons

scrap fabric

SUPPLIES:

· Iron
· White cotton or
  linen handkerchief
· Pencil and paper
  (for sketching)
· Fabric crayons
· Tape (optional)
· Scrap piece of
  fabric
· Envelope
· Waxed cord or
  ribbon
· Gift tags

tip
This also makes
a great gift idea for
Father's Day and
even birthdays
by simply changing
the drawing
and the greetings
on the tag.

STEPS:

1. Ask an adult to IRON the handkerchief.

2. SKETCH your drawing on paper as practice; then DRAW it directly on the handkerchief with the fabric crayons. To keep the cloth steady, have someone HOLD the corners or TAPE them down.

3. PLACE a scrap piece of fabric over the drawing, and gently IRON according to the instructions on the crayon package to set the design and make it permanent.

4. FOLD the handkerchief so that it will fit in an envelope with the design centered on top, and TIE it loosely with waxed cord or thin ribbon, adding a gift tag.

FELT PINS AND BARRETTES

Festive holly pins are easy to make in multiples, so you can make one for yourself and dozens for your friends. Fasten the accessories to personalized cards for easy giving.

color scheme

Have fun with color: True holly leaves are green, but yours can be made of any color felt you like. Combine the leaves with contrasting ribbons and ornaments— jewel tones are especially pretty at the holidays.

card stock

pins

barrettes

felt

ornaments

ribbon

tinsel

scissors

glue gun

SUPPLIES:

- Scissors
- Felt Pins and Barrettes template (see page 341)
- Wool felt
- Iron
- Disappearing-ink fabric pen
- Low-temperature glue gun
- Ball ornaments, tiny pom-poms, and bits of tinsel and ribbon, for trimmings
- Pins and barrettes
- Colored card stock
- Hole punch
- Rubber tag stamp
- White ink pad

STEPS:

1. CUT out the template. From a piece of felt, cut one 2½-by-5-inch rectangle for each pair of leaves. FOLD rectangle in half lengthwise. An adult should CREASE felt with an iron set to "wool." With the rectangle still folded, TRACE the template with the fabric pen and CUT out the shape using scissors. UNFOLD.

2. To make the 4-leaf design, CROSS 2 felt shapes; using the glue gun, ATTACH at the center. For the 2-leaf version, DAB glue at the center of 1 felt shape and FOLD, angling the leaves.

3. GLUE desired trimmings to the front and a bar pin or a barrette to the back.

4. To prepare as a gift: CUT a 4-by-5-inch piece of card stock. PUNCH 2 small holes, about 1 inch apart, into the center of the card. ATTACH the pin or barrette. Using a rubber stamp and a white ink pad, STAMP a "tag" with space for a name and greeting.

HEART-IN-HAND COOKIES

A little hand can double as a pattern for shaping sugar cookies. A sanding-sugar heart is sprinkled on just before baking. Package each cookie in a ribbon-tied waxed-paper bag backed with blue glassine; include a hand-drawn greeting if desired.

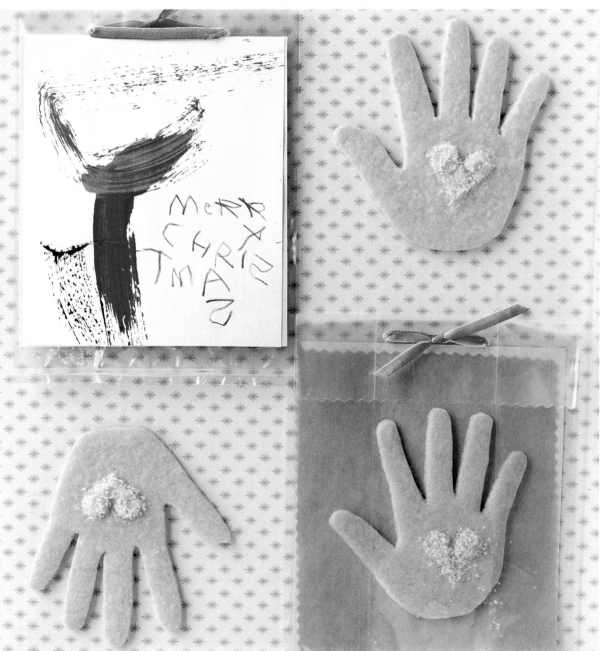

to make the cookie dough

INGREDIENTS:

- 2 cups sifted all-purpose flour, plus more for dusting
- ¼ teaspoon salt
- ½ teaspoon baking powder
- 8 tablespoons (1 stick) unsalted butter, softened
- 1 cup granulated sugar
- 1 large egg
- 1 teaspoon pure vanilla extract

DIRECTIONS:

1. Into a large bowl, sift together flour, salt, and baking powder. With an electric mixer on medium speed, beat the butter and granulated sugar until fluffy, about 3 minutes. Add whole egg, and beat until smooth, about 1 minute.

2. Add flour mixture, and mix on low speed just until thoroughly combined. Mix in vanilla. Wrap dough in plastic, and chill until firm, at least 3 hours (or overnight). MAKES ENOUGH FOR 8 TO 10 HAND COOKIES

SUPPLIES:

- Cookie Dough recipe and ingredients (above)
- Scissors
- 2 large baking sheets
- Parchment
- Flour, for dusting
- Rolling pin
- Wooden skewer
- Paring knife
- Large egg white mixed with 1 teaspoon water, for egg wash
- Pastry brush
- Sanding sugar
- Wire cooling rack
- Metal spatula

STEPS:

1. Make a heart stencil while wrapped dough is chilling: CUT out a small heart shape from a piece of parchment, discarding heart.

2. PREHEAT oven to 325°F. LINE 2 large baking sheets with parchment. On a well-floured work surface, ROLL out chilled dough to ⅛ inch thick. TRACE around child's hand with a wooden skewer, then CUT out with a paring knife.

3. TRANSFER hand shapes to prepared baking sheets. CHILL until firm, about 30 minutes (to help them hold their shape). Dough scraps may be rerolled twice to CUT out more cookies.

4. LAY the heart stencil over a chilled hand shape. BRUSH the egg wash inside the heart, and sprinkle with sanding sugar. Carefully LIFT stencil and REPEAT with remaining cookies.

5. BAKE until edges just begin to brown lightly, rotating sheets halfway through, 8 to 10 minutes. Let cookies cool on sheets for 3 minutes before using a spatula to TRANSFER to a wire rack to cool completely. (Cookies will keep at room temperature up to 1 week in an airtight container.)

BUTTON ORNAMENTS

Buttons are inexpensive and a cinch to work with. Stack them to make one of these Christmas charmers: There's Santa with a white felt beard and black button boots, a snowman with a wide-brimmed button hat, and a reindeer with a red nose. The Santa and snowman instructions are on page 316; you can use the same technique outlined there to make other characters, like the pair of green elves. Tuck them inside tiny gift boxes.

HOW-TO

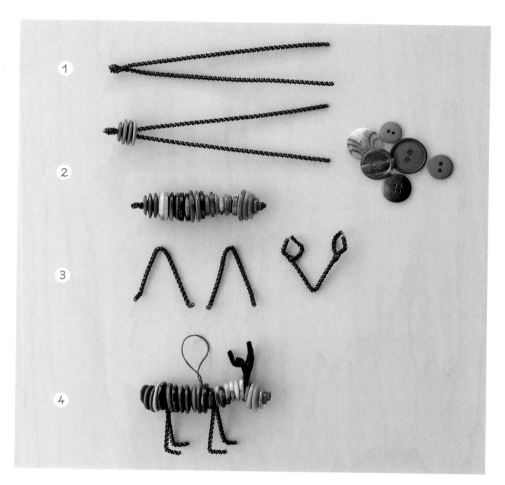

SUPPLIES:

- Pipe cleaners in various colors
- Buttons in various colors and sizes
- Scissors
- Embroidery floss
- Glue
- Felt

to make a reindeer

1. BEND a brown pipe cleaner in half and TWIST at the top.

2. SLIDE buttons onto pipe cleaner, slipping one end into each hole (if button has 4 holes, use 2 diagonal ones). SECURE buttons at end by trimming and bending pipe cleaners.

3. To add legs and antlers, BEND pieces of pipe cleaner in half, SLIP in place between buttons, and twist to secure.

4. To hang, LOOP embroidery floss around its middle and tie.

BUTTON ORNAMENTS HOW-TO

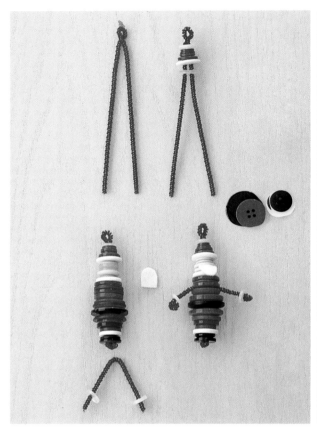

to make a santa

Bend a red pipe cleaner in half, twisting once at top to make a loop for hanging. Slide on buttons, using larger ones for his belly. Secure buttons at end by trimming and bending pipe cleaner. To add arms, bend a piece of red pipe cleaner in half and curl up ends for hands; wrap a short piece of white pipe cleaner around each hand for a cuff. Glue on a piece of white felt for a beard.

to make a snowman

Bend a black pipe cleaner in half, twisting once at top to make a loop for hanging. Slide on buttons, using larger ones for a belly and hat brim. Secure buttons at end by trimming and bending pipe cleaner. Glue on a triangle of orange felt for a nose.

BUTTON CARDS

Atop pieces of folded card stock, construction paper cutouts and snips of ribbon help turn a round of green buttons into a wreath, tiny red ones into holly berries, and stacked white buttons of graduated sizes into a friendly snowman. Mark placement of buttons and other pieces before attaching with white craft glue; hang with lengths of thin satin ribbon, if desired.

TOOLS AND MATERIALS

Stocking up on some tools and supplies will ensure that you can make any of the projects in this book whenever the mood strikes—and can inspire hours of rewarding activity. Start with the basics (scissors, pencils and markers, glue, etc.) and then add some more specialized tools as you build your crafting skills and experience.

TOOLS

adult supervision! These tools require help from an adult. Please do not use them without supervision!

stapler Sometimes the classics work best—use this one to join sheets of paper.

kids' scissors The safest ones for kids are the kind with the rounded tips.

pinking shears Prevent cut fabric from fraying by giving it a zigzag edge with these shears. They are also great for paper (they have a longer reach than decorative-edge scissors)—but use separate pairs for fabric and paper.

all-purpose scissors It's a good idea to designate one pair for paper and another for fabric and ribbon. Paper dulls the blades, so those shears won't work as well if you use them on fabric, and can even damage the cloth.

hole punch A traditional hole punch is still the best tool for making a neat hole at the edge of a piece of paper. The classic shape is a circle, but you'll also find hearts, stars, holiday symbols, and more, plus mini and micro punches for extra-small holes.

utility knives Also known as craft knives, these very sharp tools cut clean, precise edges. They are excellent for cutting heavier papers, cardboard, and foam core but not recommended for tissue paper or flimsy fabric, both of which will tear easily. Always make sure utility knives are handled by adults, and use a sharp blade.

 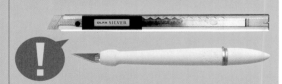

ruler For precision, reach for a ruler. Use it for measuring and marking dimensions on paper and for fabric, and for help in making straight lines.

SEWING TOOLS

pins Different lengths, thicknesses, and head styles of pins are useful for various projects. Colorful ball-head pins are easy to see and handle. Choose fine pins for sheer, delicate fabrics, and thicker ones for heavier fabrics.

embroidery and sewing needles An all-purpose, medium-size sewing needle is essential for hand-sewing. Needle sizes are numbered: 1 is the largest, and 12 the smallest. The most common hand-sewing needles are called sharps; use blunt, or ball-point, needles for knit fabrics. Embroidery needles have larger eyes, for easier threading of floss or yarn.

MEDIUMS

colored pencils Sharpen them to draw thin lines, or hold so the tip lies flat to shade larger areas and to create leaf rubbings.

permanent markers These work well on many surfaces that other markers don't, such as plastic and metal. As the name implies, the ink is permanent, so keep them out of reach of young kids. If you use these markers on paper, be sure to cover your work surface, as the ink bleeds through pages.

crayons Besides being fun for coloring, crayons can be used as a wax resist to create designs on Easter eggs—draw on the eggs, then dye them for color contrasts.

markers Markers are a classic crafts essential. They are available in every imaginable color and in a variety of widths, as well as with several types of ink. Washable markers are a smart choice for kids' crafts.

graphite pencils These school tools are indispensible for making marks you'll want to erase later.

disappearing-ink fabric pen Use this for marking fabric—the ink washes away easily. Unlike chalk, it can be used on both light and dark cloth.

tempera paint This kid-friendly nontoxic paint is good for paper and posters, and dries quickly.

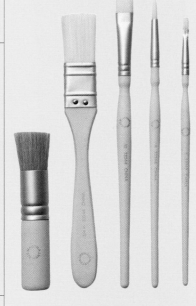

acrylic paint Available in a wide range of colors, acrylic paint works well on many surfaces and is good for precision detail work as well as broader strokes.

paintbrushes A soft, white nylon-bristle brush is great for most crafts. Brushes with round bases and pointed tips paint finer lines. To paint a broad line quickly or to color large areas, use a flat brush. Brushes with easy-to-grip thick handles are best for younger kids.

stamps and ink pad Press these stamps into colorful inks and use them to add words, numerals, shapes, and other artistic details to papers and fabrics. For use with rubber stamps, ink pads are available in an almost endless range of colors, and with different types of ink, including fabric ink.

ADHESIVES

school glue This basic glue is compatible with most craft materials, including paper, cardboard, felt, and glitter; it does not have as strong a bond as white craft glue (right). The relatively thinner consistency makes it easy to spread, but it's not the best choice for precise work. Diluted glue stops fabric edges from fraying.

glue stick With a glue stick, you can bond pieces of paper—even thin ones—to each other with little mess. This glue dries very quickly, so it's best for smaller areas. Acid-free glue will not deteriorate over time.

white craft glue The go-to glue! All-purpose white glue, such as Sobo, works on paper, wood, felt, and more. It has a thicker consistency and stronger bond than school glue.

tacky glue Its thick consistency makes this glue good for holding heavier items, such as buttons and beads. It can also be used as a cool, safe alternative to a hot-glue gun in many projects.

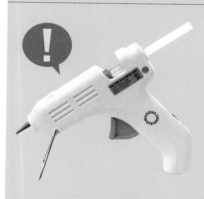

clear tape This office basic is especially useful for crafting because it can be removed easily from most surfaces.

double-sided tape A mess-free adhesive for small crafts when you don't need the bond of glue—and don't want the tape to show. This works well for paper crafts and scrapbook projects because it doesn't cause paper to buckle, as glue might. Look for archival and photo-safe varieties.

hot glue gun To join porous and nonporous materials, use a hot-glue gun. The glue and the applicator tip can burn, so be sure to keep a bowl of cool water on hand while working with one. The tool comes in high-, low-, and dual-temperature models (the higher the temperature, the stronger the bond).

masking tape This is removable, so you can paint along its edge and peel it off to make straight lines; use it to affix protective paper to a work surface while you craft; or use it to temporarily hold something in place while you're mapping out a design. Colored versions are also decorative—use them for stripes or other accents.

PAPERS

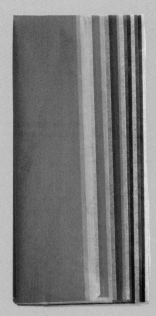

newsprint Rolls and large pads of this paper are inexpensive and handy for drawing, painting, and block printing.

construction and copier paper You'll reach for these basic papers again and again. Construction paper fades easily, so don't use it for projects that you intend to display in a sunny spot, or to keep for many years.

origami paper Available in countless patterns, colors, and subtle textures, origami paper is square, thin, and very easy to fold. It's nice for collages and comes in a variety of sizes.

tissue paper This is great for wrapping presents or as filler inside a gift bag. To punch shapes from tissue paper, stack three sheets with a sheet of plain paper, which acts as a stiffener, and punch through all four layers. This is the easiest way to make confetti (also good for making paper flowers and pom-poms).

crepe paper Sturdy and stretchy but lightweight, crepe paper can be sewn or ironed with a dry iron. It is sold in solid-colored sheets (called folds). Double-sided crepe paper (different colors on either side) is also available, but less common.

kraft paper Roll out kraft paper to protect a work surface, make it the background for a large drawing or painting, or use it as gift wrap. It's also good for making templates or patterns for sewing.

card stock and scrapbooking paper Card stock is called for when you need a piece of paper that is stiff and sturdy. It's worth keeping sheets in different hues on hand. Scrapbooking paper comes in many different colors, patterns, and even themed designs; it's normally sold in tablets/pads.

vellum Translucent paper that comes in many colors, vellum is excellent for making cards. Printable vellum is available. Be aware that over-folding can crack the paper.

MATERIALS

yarn Whether or not you knit, yarn is fun to craft with; create pom-poms, dolls' hair, and other project details. The label on a skein of yarn will tell you about the fiber content and care instructions.

pipe cleaners Also called chenille stems, these are a craft staple. Twist them into fuzzy animal shapes and so much more.

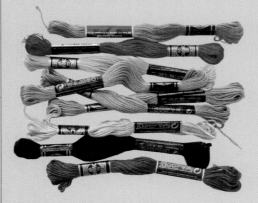

embroidery thread A must for friendship bracelets! Every strand of embroidery thread, also called embroidery floss, is made of several thinner strands. It comes in a wide range of colors.

thread Keep several colors on hand in a sewing kit so you'll have what you need to match your project.

baker's twine and string Food-safe twine is excellent for wrapping gifts and baked goods, and for making cards and garlands. It comes in large quantities for reasonable prices.

ribbon For so much more than wrapping gifts, ribbon is a versatile trimming that finishes off many projects. Always save ribbons that come on packages and add them to your collection for future crafting.

felt This soft cloth doesn't fray, so it's a breeze to work with—no hemming required. We like 100% wool felt, but synthetic versions are fine for many tasks (and more economical).

pom-poms They come in a range of sizes and colors. Use as is to adorn gifts and cards, or create a menagerie of fuzzy pom-pom animals.

buttons Fabric stores sell an inspiring array, but it's fun to look for buttons at tag sales—you can pick them up for pennies. Buttons may be made out of plastic, wood, leather, glass, mother-of-pearl, and other materials, in a rainbow of colors and assorted shapes and sizes. Add any spare buttons to your collection.

glitter The shimmery material comes in a range of colors and sizes, from fine powdered glitter to more confetti-like sizes and shapes. Glitter can be messy, so it's a good idea to work over a surface (such as a glitter tray) that catches the excess to make cleanup easier—you can put the glitter back in the container to reuse.

seed beads Tiny round beads (2.5–3mm is a good size range) are obviously good for beading projects, but they also make excellent accents—use them as facial features on animal figures, for example. The tiny size makes them better for older kids and adults to use.

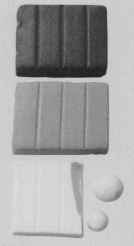

wood beads These tend to be large enough for smaller hands to thread; look for interesting shapes and textures.

sequins For kids, sequins can act as a larger form of glitter to add some sparkle to a craft project.

polymer clay
This is a moldable clay that hardens when you bake it (grown-ups, of course, have to help when it's time to use the oven). You'll find baking instructions on the package.

HOUSEHOLD ITEMS

Keep a good stock of these and other recycled items on hand for all sorts of crafting projects.

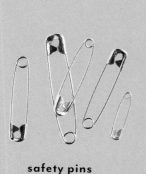

safety pins

tin cans

bottle caps

craft sticks

paper-towel tubes

egg cartons

EXTRA LARGE

SOURCES

The following is a list of vendors our editors rely on again and again for tools, materials, and other crafts supplies. Addresses, phone numbers, and websites were verified at the time of publication and are subject to change.

General Crafts Supplies

Stitch Craft Create
0844 880 5852
www.stitchcraftcreate.co.uk

Hobbycrafts
0800 027 2387
www.hobbycraft.co.uk

Craft Creations
01992 781 900
www.craftcreations.com

Panduro Hobby
0845 121 6875
www.panduro.co.uk

Dylon
01737 742 020
www.dylon.co.uk

Ikea
www.ikea.com

Homecrafts Direct
0116 269 7733
www.homecrafts.co.uk

Paper, Cards, and Stationery

Stitch Craft Create
0844 880 5852
www.stitchcraftcreate.co.uk

The Paper Warehouse
0153 972 6161
www.ghpkendal.co.uk

Paperchase
020 7467 6200
www.paperchase.co.uk

The Craft Barn
01342 836 398
www.craftbarnonline.co.uk

The Art of Craft
01252 377 677
www.art-of-craft.co.uk

Jane Jenkins Quilling Design
01482 843 721
www.jjquilling.co.uk

Fred Aldous Ltd
0161 236 4224
www.fredaldous.co.uk

Calico Crafts
01353 624 100
www.calicocrafts.co.uk

Packing

Online Packaging Shop
0845 071 0079
www.onlinepackagingshop.co.uk

Beads and Jewelry-Making Supplies
(including chains, charms, clasps, and jump rings)

Beads Direct
0870 086 9877
www.beadsdirect.co.uk

The Bead Scene
01327 353 639
www.thebeadscene.com

Kars
01844 238 080
www.kars.biz

Gutermann
020 8589 1600
www.guetermann.com

Stitch Craft Create
0844 880 5852
www.stitchcraftcreate.co.uk

The Spellbound Bead Company
01543 417 650
www.spellboundbead.co.uk

The Bead Shop
020 7240 0931
www.beadworks.co.uk

Creative Beadcraft Ltd
01494 778 818
www.creativebeadcraft.co.uk

Ribbon, Cord, and Twine

Stitch Craft Create
0844 880 5852
www.stitchcraftcreate.co.uk

Crafts U Love
01293 863 576
www.craftsulove.co.uk

Crafty Ribbons
01258 455 889
www.craftyribbons.com

Rope Locker
0117 230 8525
www.ropelocker.co.uk

Yarn

Designer Yarns Ltd
01535 664 222
www.designeryarns.uk.com

Rowan
01484 681 881
www.knitrowan.com

Sirdar Spinning Ltd
01924 371501
www.sirdar.co.uk

Stitch Craft Create
0844 880 5852
www.stitchcraftcreate.co.uk

Candy and Sprinkles

The Cake Parlour
020 8947 4424
www.thecakeparlour.com

The Candy Can Co.
01382 360 640
www.thecandycancompany.com

Stitch Craft Create
0844 880 5852
www.stitchcraftcreate.co.uk

The Sugar Shack
020 8204 2994
www.sugarshack.co.uk

Squire's Kitchen Shop
0845 617 1810
www.squires-shop.com

TEMPLATES

On the following pages, you'll find images of most of the templates and clip art included in the book. Unless otherwise directed, copy the templates at 100 percent, or size to your project as needed. Go to marthastewart.com/kids-crafts-book-extras to download these and other templates and clip art.

paper bag puppets, page 22
(enlarge 180%)

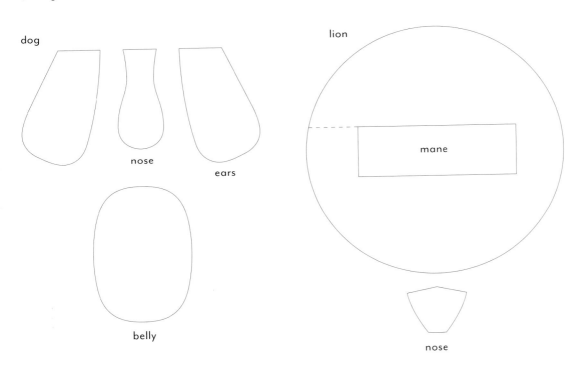

dog

nose

ears

belly

lion

mane

nose

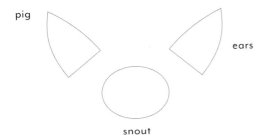

pig

ears

snout

beak

ear

rooster's comb

monkey's
ear

foot or paw

monkey's
face

bee's wing

mane

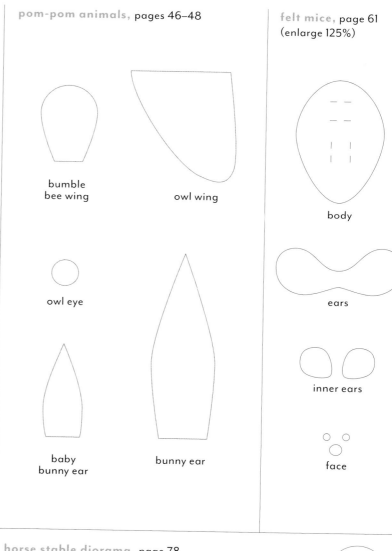

bumble
bee wing

owl wing

owl eye

baby
bunny ear

bunny ear

body

ears

inner ears

face

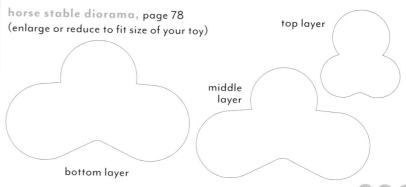

top layer

middle
layer

bottom layer

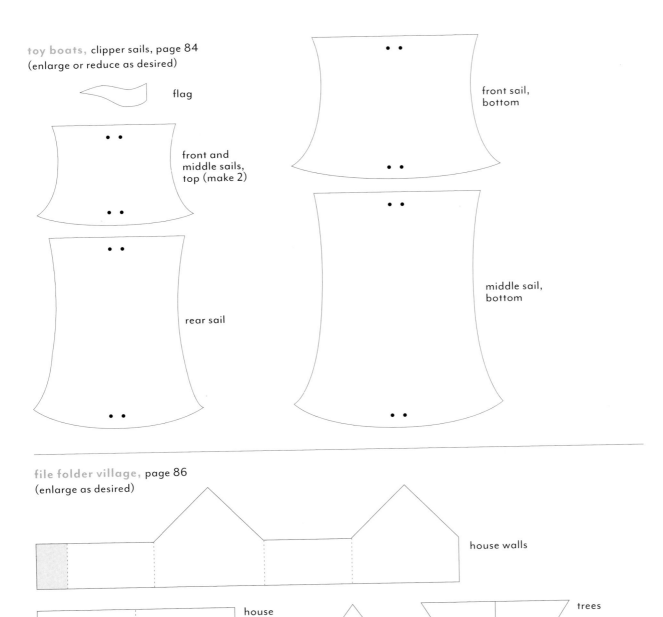

toy boats, clipper sails, page 84
(enlarge or reduce as desired)

flag

front and
middle sails,
top (make 2)

front sail,
bottom

rear sail

middle sail,
bottom

file folder village, page 86
(enlarge as desired)

house walls

house
roof

trees

cardboard worlds, page 100
(enlarge as desired; ours were 13" by 9" and 19" by 9")

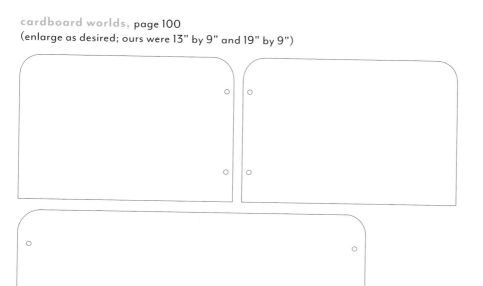

bingo!, page 136
(download the full set at marthastewart.com/kids-crafts-books-extras and print at full size)

B	I	N	G	O
1	9	15	20	26
3	10	13	22	29
5	8	FREE	24	30
2	11	17	23	28
4	12	18	19	27

B	I	N	G	O
3	12	13	19	29
5	11	17	20	30
2	7	FREE	22	28
4	10	18	24	27
1	9	15	23	26

gingham dolls, **page 142**
(enlarge 400%)

girl

mom

baby

boy

dad

beastly mittens, page 174

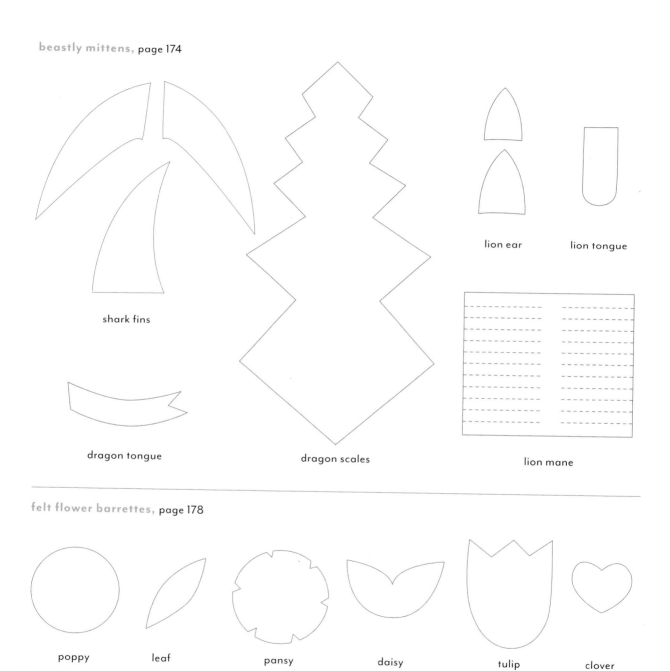

shark fins

dragon tongue

dragon scales

lion ear

lion tongue

lion mane

felt flower barrettes, page 178

poppy

leaf

pansy

daisy

tulip

clover

superhero costumes, letters and symbol for cape and T-shirt, page 194
(enlarge 400%)

ABCDE

FGHIJK

LMNOP

QRSTUV

WXYZ ⚡

superhero costumes, pages 196 and 197
(enlarge 150%)

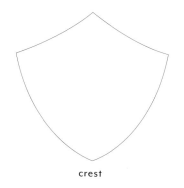

crest

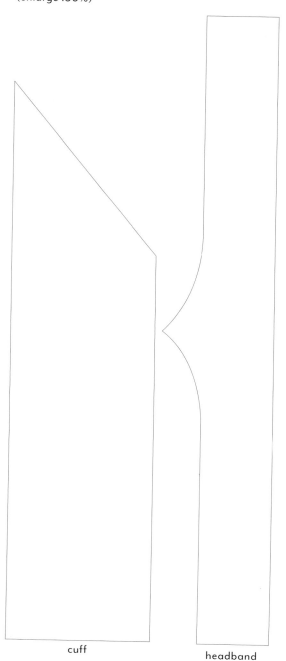

cuff

headband

weather watching, wind vane bird, page 219
(enlarge 200%)

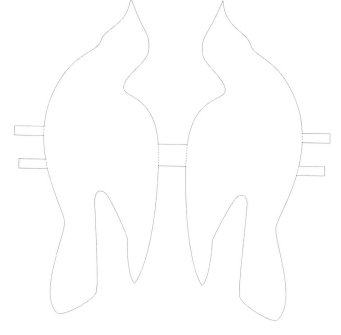

movie magic, thaumatrope images, page 237
(enlarge 133%)

movie magic, phenakistoscope disk, page 239
(enlarge 133%)

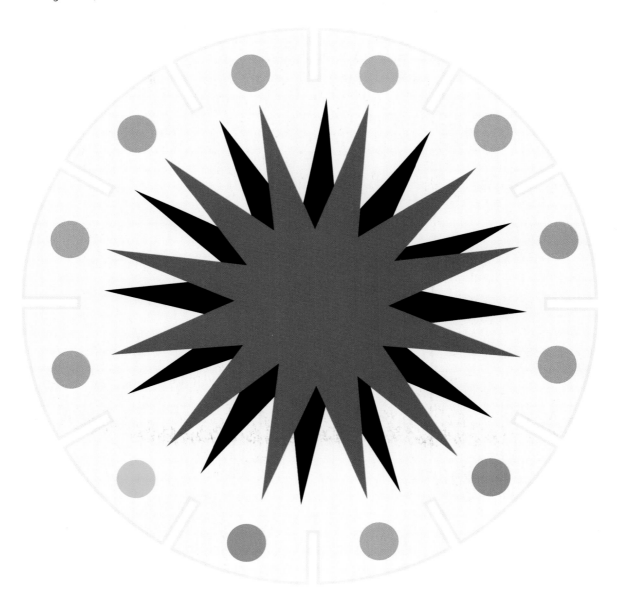

cross-stitch family portraits, page 268
(download at marthastewart.com/kids-crafts-book-extras)

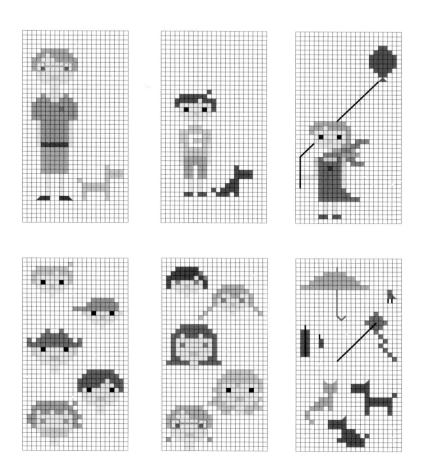

bottle piggy banks,
page 259

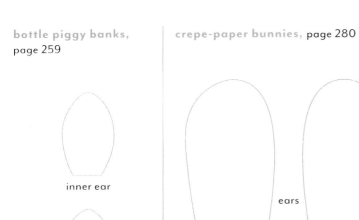

inner ear

outer ear

crepe-paper bunnies, page 280

ears

eyelashes

nose

baby-chick beanbags, page 282

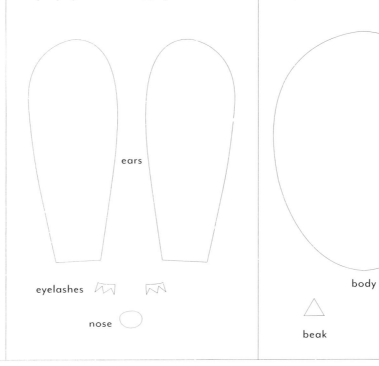

body

beak

wing

july 4th rocket favors, page 292
(enlarge 287%)

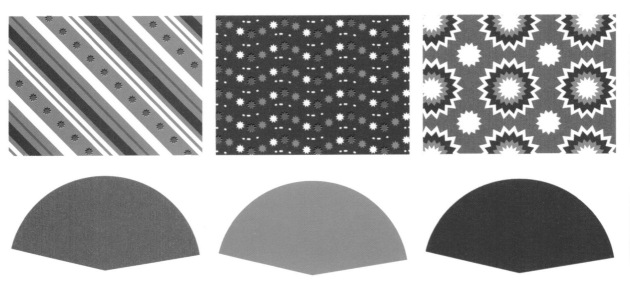

halloween favor
tree, page 294

ghoulish goodies, page 298

felt pins and barrettes, page 310

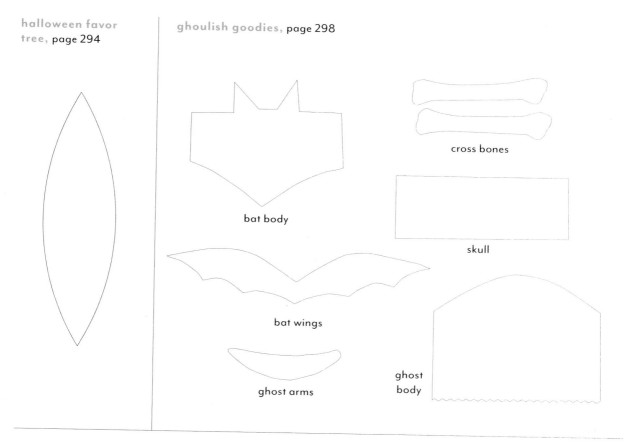

cross bones

bat body

skull

bat wings

ghost arms

ghost
body

PHOTO CREDITS

William Abranowicz: 224–229

Antonis Achilleos: 273

Sang An: 22–23, 30, 32–35, 50–55, 66–67, 126, 128 (left), 129, 182–183, 188, 216- 219, 257

James Baigrie: 24, 180 , 181 (left), 252, 256, 260–265, 275, 306–307

Harry Bates Illustration: 144–145, 153 (top), 155 (top), 157 (top), 181 (top right and bottom right)

Monica Buck: 176–177, 234–235, 258

Jennifer Causey: 268–271

Susie Cushner: 279, 314–317

Aaron Dyer: 259

Dwight Eschliman: 56–57

Formula Z/S: 65

Laurie Frankel: 139

Dana Gallagher: 142–143

Bryan Gardner: 60, 204, 274, 309, 318 (bottom right), 319 (colored pencils, crayons, markers, and graphite pencils), 320 (tempera paint, paintbrushes, acrylic paint, and rubber stamps), 321 (glue gun, clear tape, and masking tape), 323 (all except pipe cleaners), 324 (all except pom-poms), 325 (top left, top middle, top right, paper-towel tubes, tin can, and craft sticks)

Gentl & Hyers: 6, 36–39, 78–79, 94–95, 136–137, 170–172, 245, 247–249, 255

Thayer Allyson Gowdy: 110–113

Frank Heckers: 205 (right)

Raymond Hom: 318 (top left and top right), 319 (sewing tools), 320 (top left), 321 (top right), 322 (crepe paper, origami paper, bottom right, and bottom left), 325 (safety pins)

Lisa Hubbard: 250, 253, 290–291

Devon Jarvis: 283

John Kernick: 230–231

Yunhee Kim: 87, 289

Sivan Lewin: 40–43

Stephen Lewis: cover spine, 16–21, 26–29, 72–77, 80–85, 88–89, 91–93, 118–123, 138, 210–212, 220–221, 236–241

Kate Mathis: 146–147

Maura McEvoy: 140

Ellie Miller: 296–297

Johnny Miller: 62–63, 132–133, 280, 302–303, 310–311, 318 (hole punch and utility knives), 319 (permanent marker), 320 (ink pad), 321 (glue stick, white craft glue, and double-sided tape), 322 (tissue paper)

Gregory Nemec Illustration: 90

Amy Neunsinger: 246

Ulla Nyeman: 58–59, 312–313

Con Poulos: 96, 98–99

Tosca Radigonda: 190–193

Manuel Rodriguez: 97

Emily Kate Roemer: 281, 292–293, 299

Hector Sanchez: 298

Lucy Schaeffer: 148–151

Charles Schiller: 158, 160–161, 308

Annie Schlechter: front cover, back cover, 1–5, 9, 10, 12, 14, 44–49, 61, 68, 70–71, 86, 100–103, 124, 130–131, 134–135, 141, 162–163, 174–175, 178–179, 184, 186, 187 (left), 198–200, 201 (top two), 202–203, 205 (left), 206–208, 214–215, 233, 242, 244, 251, 254, 266, 272, 277, 284–288, 300–301, 304–305, 321 (top left), 327, 343, 351–352

Tamara Schlesinger: 194–197

Victor Schrager: 104, 106–109, 152, 153 (bottom), 154, 155 (bottom), 156, 157 (bottom), 213, 222–223, 232

Bill Steele: 164–165

Laura Stojanovic: 318 (scissors and ruler), 322 (newsprint, construction and copier paper, and kraft paper), 323 (top left), 324 (bottom middle), 325 (sequins, egg carton, and bottle caps)

Kirsten Strecker: 294–295

Anna Williams: 25, 31, 64, 114–117, 166–169, 276, 278, 282

INDEX

ABOUT THE AUTHOR

Martha Stewart is America's most trusted lifestyle expert and teacher and is the author of more than 75 books, including the bestselling *Martha Stewart's Encyclopedia of Crafts, Martha Stewart's Encyclopedia of Sewing and Fabric Crafts,* and *Martha Stewart's Handmade Holiday Crafts.* Her namesake company, Martha Stewart Living Omnimedia, publishes *Martha Stewart Living* magazine and *Martha Stewart Weddings* and has a growing retail presence with 8,500 products in thousands of retail locations, including a full line of crafts products at Michaels and Jo-Ann Fabric and Craft Stores. Martha especially enjoys spending time with her two grandchildren, and she looks forward to many hours spent crafting with them.

www.marthastewart.com